Learning to Think

BOOKS BY E. R. EMMET

BRAIN PUZZLER'S DELIGHT (PUBLISHED IN ENGLAND
AS "101 BRAIN PUZZLERS)"

PUZZLES FOR PLEASURE

MIND TICKLING BRAIN TEASERS

Learning to Think

E. R. EMMET
Formerly Assistant Master, Winchester College

EMERSON BOOKS, INC.
Verplanck, New York 10596

© *E. R. Emmet, 1965*, 1980
Second American Printing , 1981

Published by Emerson Books, Inc.
Standard Book Number 87523-195.0
Library of Congress Catalog Card Number 80-65503

Contents

Preface

The purpose of this book is explained in its title. It is a purpose which one might expect to be generally regarded as educationally important. But in this country in recent years, although many teachers of different subjects might claim perfectly correctly that to think more clearly is an essential part of what they teach, there does not seem to have been much attempt to teach clear thinking by a direct method. This appears to have been due to a general feeling that logic, the formal study of correct thinking, has become too remote and too difficult for the ordinary man. The logicians, it might be said, have in a sense tried too hard. In their search for certainty or necessity they have lost touch with reality, and have increasingly concentrated their attention on closed-system logical games.

It is my opinion that all the thinking which we do or may want to do can be made clearer and simpler by a study of the basic principles. And one of the most important of these principles seems to me to be that in most of this thinking certainty or necessity is not attainable. To realise this will help us to understand more fully the possible objectives and to avoid the frustration and the twisting of our thinking that may result from an attempt to attain what is in principle unattainable, logical necessity in the world of contingent events.

There may well be doubt about the age at which this book should be used. In my view there is much to be said for teaching the principles of clear thinking, which necessarily include much about the proper way to handle language, when the mind is at its most active and pliable, say at about the age of 15. But this is not to imply that it cannot be profitably studied at any age after this, or even in some cases before. The closed-system logical problems, for which no background knowledge or experience are required, may be tackled as effectively by the intelligent child of 13 as by almost anyone. And I have often been surprised at the determination and success with which those who were not generally regarded as particularly intelligent have dealt with them. Many of the open-system problems are likely to lead to the kind of discussion that can be profitable at a variety of levels.

I am grateful to many friends with whom I have discussed the content and the method of this book and who have tried out some of the exercises. I mention with particular gratitude for many helpful comments and suggestions Miss Hazel Eardley-Wilmot. My thanks also once again to Mrs J. H. Preston for the skill and accuracy with which she typed from my unattractive manuscript the whole of this book and the companion volume. And, most of all, my gratitude to my wife for her unfailing encouragement and support and the wisdom of her comment and criticism.

E. R. E.

Chapter 1

Introduction - Two Systems of Thinking

We all think. We talk, we write, we draw conclusions, we argue and reason. We use sentences like 'If so and so, then such and such', 'Because of this, therefore that must follow'. But most people have not really been taught very much about how thinking or reasoning works. One is supposed, rather oddly, just to pick it up. If an argument is wildly irrational it will be obvious to most people that it does not follow. 'If Tom is older than John, then Tom can't be John's father', must clearly be wrong, and no one would find it difficult to explain why. 'Because Liverpool is bigger than Manchester, therefore Taunton is smaller than Bristol', looks like a completely nonsensical argument, though it is possible that for the speaker the information that Liverpool was bigger than Manchester was the last link enabling him to arrive at his conclusion. (For example, he might have been told that so far as size is concerned Liverpool was to Manchester as Bristol was to Taunton.)

If people picked up the principles of reasoning in such a way as to be able to detect what arguments were wrong and why, and to be able to argue correctly themselves, everything would clearly be entirely satisfactory. But that is unfortunately and obviously not the case. We all make mistakes in reasoning and most of us know it. We very often have the strong feeling (though it is not necessarily a correct one) that something is very wrong with that argument, but we can't quite see what. It seems likely that we should stand a better chance of thinking correctly and clearly ourselves, and of distinguishing between correct and incorrect thinking in others, if we studied rather more closely the basic principles of reasoning.

To do this is the objective of this book. In this introductory chapter we shall make some basic points and distinctions and take a broad survey of the ground we intend to cover.

LOGIC

The study of the basic principles of reasoning is usually called 'logic'. Since the time of Aristotle (about 384–322 B.C.) logic as a subject has been studied by learned people, but on the whole more at universities than in schools. In recent times there has been a tendency to think of it as something abstruse and difficult, closely connected with pure mathematics, but not having very much to do with our day-to-day reasoning. We shall try very hard here to keep the exposition of the principles of thinking in touch with the realities of everyday living. Logic has tended more and more to become a formal closed system, shut off from experience. But it is as they are applied to the world of experience, the world in which we live, that it is most important and useful to study the principles of reasoning.

CLOSED SYSTEMS

The distinction which we make between a 'closed' system of thinking and an 'open' one is of considerable importance. We illustrate the difference by considering a simple puzzle.

'Litt, Mitt and Nitt were born, not respectively, in Lapland, Mapland, and Napland and they now live, again not respectively, in Lod, Mod and Nod. For each of them the initial letters of his name, his country of birth and his country of residence are all different. Litt has never been to Nod. Find where they were all born and where they all live.'

It is obvious that this is an artificial problem, and no one would be likely to look Mitt up in the telephone directory in order to ring him up and ask him where he was born. It can be done by simple inference using only the data that is given and that data cannot be changed by events. It would clearly be irrelevant and foolish to start wondering whether perhaps Mitt has now moved. The system is closed, insulated from what is happening in the world of experience, and the same problem could have been set in a large number of different ways.[1]

In solving this and similar problems it is often helpful to eliminate

[1] The reasoning required for the solution is as follows: Litt has never been to Nod and since his country and his name cannot begin with the same letter he cannot live in Lod. Therefore he must live in *Mod*. And since his name, his country of birth and his country of residence all begin with different letters he must have been born in *Napland*. Mitt therefore cannot have been born in Napland; nor can he have been born in Mapland (because of the

what is impossible and take what is left. This is a method that also has important applications to our thinking in an open system. But it is a method that is often curiously neglected; we are so anxious to find out what the answer *is*, that it does not occur to us to help ourselves by thinking what it is *not*.

An 'open' system is one that is part of, or in touch with, the world of experience, our everyday practical living. The distinction between the two will not be entirely clearcut; we shall find many cases where we are thinking partly in a closed and partly in an open system. But it is a useful distinction to make, and one of the most important features about it, as we shall see in more detail later, is the difference in the degree or kind of certainty which attaches to conclusions in the two systems.

There are many examples of closed systems of thinking: pure mathematics; games like draughts, bridge and chess. And it is always easy to devise more, especially once one has gained a certain facility in the manipulation of symbols. These systems may then become alarmingly complicated, as in the upper reaches of formal logic.

It is obvious that much of the thinking that is done in these closed systems is exceedingly difficult. A chess master on any reckoning is a very clever person. Dealing with these systems exercises the mind, and many people get a great deal of enjoyment from it. There may, however, sometimes be some doubt as to the extent to which the exercising of the mind in a closed system, where the answers are necessary and certain, is of much assistance when it comes to dealing with open system problems. It may indeed be argued that the individual who attacks open system problems with a mind that has been rigorously and almost exclusively trained in the necessities of a closed system may be at a positive disadvantage.

Nevertheless quite a lot of the thinking and problems in this book will be with the assumptions of a closed system. It is helpful to some extent to study basic principles with the door temporarily shut on the outside world. What is important is that the door should subsequently be opened and that we should understand what difference its opening makes, to what extent the principles of reasoning

initial letters); therefore he was born in *Lapland* and therefore he must live in *Nod*. Nitt therefore must have been born in *Mapland* and he must live in *Lod*.

studied in a closed system have to be qualified before they can be applied to an open one. Most people like the intellectual exercise that can be provided by puzzles in a closed system. If they do not it is often because they have not found themselves very good at them; perhaps with study and practice they may become better.

We will now consider a rather more complicated closed system problem.

'Smith, Brown, Jones and Robinson are told that they have each won one of the four prizes for Mathematics, English, French and Logic, but they none of them know which. They are speculating about it. Smith says he thinks Robinson has won the Logic prize. Brown thinks that Jones has won the English prize. Jones feels confident that Smith has not won the Mathematics prize, and Robinson is of the opinion that Brown has won the French prize. It turns out that the winners of the Mathematics and Logic prizes were correct in their speculations, but the other two were wrong. Who won which prize?'

As with any practical or intellectual exercise it is likely to be easier if we tackle it systematically. Any negative information that we can get about the prizes which they did not win will be helpful, and indeed the process of elimination is likely to be our most potent weapon.

It will be useful therefore to draw up a table like this:

	Maths	English	French	Logic
Smith				
Brown				
Jones				
Robinson				

If we then discover that Smith did not win the Mathematics prize we can put a X in the first column in the first row; if we discover that Smith did win the Mathematics prize we can put a √ in that position, and we can then fill up the remainder of that column and of that row with X's. For if Smith won the Mathematics prize he did not win any of the others, and the Mathematics prize was not won by anybody else.

It will then also be convenient to set down what we are told about what they say in shorthand form, using initial letters, S, B, J, R, for their names and M, E, F, L for their subjects, thus:

S	says	R	won	L
B	„	J	won	E
J	„	S did not win	M
R	„	B	won	F

And we can remind ourselves that the winners of the Mathematics and Logic prizes were correct in their speculations and that the winners of the French and English prizes were incorrect by marking the subjects in the table with √'s and X's respectively.

The difficulty will now be to find a starting point. A profitable method will be to suppose one of the speculations to be true or false and see what follows. If we get involved in a contradiction our original supposition must have been false.

We will suppose that B's speculation is correct. Then, since J won E, J's speculation is wrong. Therefore S did win M. Therefore S's speculation is correct. Therefore R won L. Therefore R's speculation is correct. Therefore B won F. Therefore B's speculation is incorrect. But this is contrary to our original supposition, which must therefore have been wrong. Therefore J did not win E, and B did not win M or L since his speculation has been shown to be wrong. X's to indicate these facts can be inserted in the table.

Suppose now that R's speculation is wrong. Then since B and R are both wrong, the other two must be right. Therefore R won L (S's speculation). But in this case R's speculation would have to be correct which is contrary to our supposition. Therefore our supposition must have been wrong and R's speculation is correct. Therefore B won F. Mark the relevant position with a √ and put X's in the rest of that row and column. Since R's speculation is correct he did not win E. In the E column there are now 3 X's. By elimination S must have won E. Therefore S's speculation is wrong and R did not win L. Therefore by elimination J won L and R won M.

Each step in this argument is quite simple and it is hoped that the reader will have followed it carefully.

There are several points which are worth noticing:

1. Each conclusion is certain; within the conditions of the problem there is no other possibility.

2. If we start with a supposition, follow its consequences and end with a conclusion that agrees with the supposition, we do not prove that the supposition is either true or false.

   Whereas if we end with a conclusion that contradicts the supposition we have proved that the supposition must be false.

   (Anyone who is not convinced of this may find the following example helpful. If we know that A is older than B and that A is older than C, the supposition that B is older than C is consistent with what we are told; but that does not prove that it is true. The supposition that B is younger than C is also consistent. But if we know that A is older than B and that B is older than C the supposition that C is older than A is *not* consistent with what we are told. It leads to a contradiction. Therefore the supposition must be false.)

3. It is unlikely that a problem of this kind would be set unless there were a solution, and that a unique one. It would of course be perfectly possible to produce a set of data that made possible either no solution or many different solutions.

The points raised by the consideration of the problems and passages in this chapter will be examined in greater detail later. What we are doing here is not learning a new discipline or subject, as though we were taking up Arabic or ballroom dancing starting from scratch, but trying to see how we can perform more effectively something that we have all done as long as we can remember, namely reasoning. To this end it is useful, before examining the basic principles very closely, to watch ourselves in action, to try out our methods, to see perhaps whether we need to examine the fundamentals more than we have done already or whether we are all right as we are. We provide therefore as we go along exercises on which the reader can test his powers. Some of them will be very easy, others will be quite hard, and it may well be that the reader will find that he will be able to tackle them more successfully after reading later chapters.

The following exercises are all closed system artificial problems. Any considerations about the events described being improbable are irrelevant. They can all be solved by common-sense processes of inference though often fairly complicated ones: some quite hard work and thinking are required. In every case there are necessary, unique solutions.

Exercises

1.1. Arthur, Basil, Charles, Douglas and Ernest are sitting round a circular table. No two men, the initial letters of whose names are next to each other in the alphabet, are next to each other at the table. Charles has Ernest's brother sitting on his right. Draw a sketch showing how everyone is sitting relative to Charles.

1.2. Three football teams A. B and C play against each other. The following table gives some information about the results.

	Played	Won	Lost	Drawn	Goals for	Goals against
A	2	2				1
B	2			1	2	4
C	2				3	7

Complete the table and find the score in each match.

1.3. Smith, Brown and Jones are speculating about which of four candidates—Conservative, Liberal, Labour, Independent—will win an election. Smith thought it would be either the Liberal or the Independent; Brown felt quite confident that it would certainly not be the Liberal candidate; and Jones expressed the opinion that neither the Independent nor the Conservative stood a chance. Only one of them was right. Who won the election?

1.4. Alpha, Beta, Gamma, Delta and Epsilon have their birthdays on consecutive days, but not necessarily in that order.
    Alpha's birthday is as many days before Gamma's as Beta's is

after Epsilon's. Delta is two days older than Epsilon. Gamma's birthday this year is on a Wednesday.

On what days of the week are the birthdays of the other four this year?

1.5. Alf, Bert, Charlie, Duggie, Ernie, Fred and George are having an argument about which day of the week it is.

They speak as follows:

ALF: The day after tomorrow is Wednesday.

BERT: No, it's Wednesday today.

CHARLIE: You're quite wrong; it's Wednesday tomorrow.

DUGGIE: Nonsense, today is neither Monday, Tuesday nor Wednesday.

ERNIE: I'm quite sure yesterday was Thursday.

FRED: No, you've got it the wrong way round. Tomorrow is Thursday.

GEORGE: Anyway yesterday was not Saturday.

Only one of these remarks is true? Which one? What day of the week is it?

1.6. In a cricket competition four teams A, B, C, D all play each other once. Points are awarded as follows:

To the side that wins: 10
To the side that wins on the first innings in a drawn match: 6
To the side that loses on the first innings in a drawn match: 2
To each side for a tie: 5
To the side that loses: 0

A, B, C, D have 21, 18, 6 and 9 points respectively. What was the result of each match?

1.7. A, B, C, D and E are involved in a competition at the end of which an order of merit is produced.

You are told that C did not win, that D was two places below E, that E was not second, that A was not first or last, and that B was one place below C.

Find the order of merit.

1.8.

No. of Question	1	2	3	4		5		Total for each person
				%	£	s	d	
A	3	20°	17	20		5	0	30
B	7	10°	21	5			2	15
C	4	18° 30′	45	5	143	0	0	30
D	3	20°	63	10			1½	
E	4	12°	21	10	17	10	0	10
Total for each Question	30	10	35	15		15		

The above table shows the answers given by five candidates A, B, C, D, E in an examination and some particulars about the total number of marks gained by each person and for each question.

If the answer was right 10 marks were given. If the answer was wrong 0 or 5 marks were given according to the method used. (If 2 people get the same wrong answer it is quite possible for one of them to get 5 and the other 0.)

At least one person got each question right. What are the right answers, and how many marks did each person get for each question?

1.9. Smith understood Mr Jones to say that the earliest time for leaving the examination room was 2 hours before lunch or 1½ hours after the examination started, whichever was the earlier. Robinson however was under the impression that Mr Jones had said that the earliest time was 2¼ hours before lunch or 1 hour after the examination started, whichever was the later.

Smith and Robinson both left the examination room at the earliest possible moment, according to what they thought their instructions were. They both left at 11.15. What can you say about the time of lunch and of the start of the examination?

1.10. In the Brown, Green, Black and White Houses live, but not respectively, the Brown, Green, Black and White families. No family lives in the house that bears its name. There is a son and daughter in each family and each son is engaged to one of the daughters, but no man is engaged to a lady who bears the same name as his family's house, and no lady is engaged to a man who bears the same name as her family's house. Mr Black's fiancée does not live at the Brown House. Mr Brown, his future brother-in-law and Mr Green were all entertained to tea at the White House.

Where does everybody live? Who is engaged to whom?

1.11. Mr and Mrs Binks, Mr and Mrs Bloggs and Mr and Mrs Bunn go to the theatre together; they sit side by side in one row with ladies and gentlemen in alternate seats. No man sits next to his wife. The men's names are John, Rupert and Ethelred; their jobs are dentist, accountant and headmaster; the names of their wives are Jane, Elizabeth, Dawn. (These names and jobs are in no particular order.)

The dentist occupies one of the middle two seats and he is sitting nearer to Dawn than he is to Mr Bloggs or to John.

Mr Binks is at one end of the row and he has the headmaster's wife on his right.

Rupert is sitting between Jane, on his left, and Elizabeth.

Find out where they are all sitting, their Christian names and the men's jobs.

1.12. Adams, Baines, Clarke, Ditheringspoon and Elliott are the only entrants for the school Spanish prize. After the result has been announced they speak as follows:

ADAMS: I was not fourth.

BAINES: I was one place lower than Clarke.

CLARKE: I won the Russian prize.

DITHERINGSPOON: I was one place higher than Adams.

ELLIOTT: I was three places higher than Clarke.

All the above remarks are true except the one that was made by the person who came last for the Spanish prize. What was the order of merit for the Spanish prize? Can you say anything about the winner of the Russian prize?

1.13. Alpha, Beta, Gamma and Omega were four young ladies of ancient Greece who were training to become oracles; in fact only one of them did and she got a post at Delphi. Of the other three one became a professional dancer, another a lady-in-waiting and the third a harp player.

During their training, when they were practising predictions one day, Alpha forecast that whatever else Beta did she would never become a professional dancer; Beta forecast that Gamma would end up as the Delphic oracle; Gamma forecast that Omega would not become a harp player; and Omega predicted that she would marry a man called Artaxerxes. The only prediction that was in fact correct was the one made by the lady who became the Delphic oracle.

Who became what? Did Omega marry Artaxerxes?

1.14. Alf, Bert, Charlie, Duggie and Ernie, the five original employees in the Utopia factory, were to be allotted the jobs of Door-Keeper, Door-Knob-Polisher, Bottle-Washer, Welfare Officer and Worker, but it was far from clear who was to do which job. They had their opinions about it, however. Alf was most emphatic that whoever was to polish the door-knobs it should not be Ernie. Charlie was very keen to wash the bottles, but Ernie thought that Duggie was the most suitable person for this job. Bert hoped that Alf would be the worker and expressed a strong disinclination himself to be the Welfare Officer. Duggie warmly recommended Bert for the job of Door-Keeper.

After the jobs had been allotted it was interesting, looking back, to see that the hopes and recommendations of the Bottle-Washer and the Worker had not in fact been fulfilled, but that those of the Door-Keeper and the Door-Knob Polisher had.

Who had which job?

1.15. In a competition between 5 football teams, A, B, C, D, E, each side is to play each of the others once.

The following table gives a certain amount of information as to what has happened after some of the matches have been played.

	Played	Won	Lost	Drawn	Goals for	Goals against
A	3	2	0		7	0
B	2	2	0		4	1
C	3	0	1		2	4
D	3	1	1		4	4
E	3	0			0	

Who has played whom? Find the result of each match and the score.

1.16. Anstruther, Banks, Clopp and Dingle are, not necessarily respectively, a Journalist, a Chauffeur, a Solicitor and a Dentist.

Banks is a cousin of the Solicitor and has often stayed with him at his home in Scotland.

Clopp is 40.

The Chauffeur is three years younger than the Journalist.

Anstruther is 35.

Dingle, who is a year younger than Banks, has lived all his life in Wales and has never driven a car.

The Solicitor is more than five years older than the Dentist.

Find their occupations and their ages.

OPEN SYSTEMS

Let us now take a look at some pieces of open system thinking.

Mrs Jones soliloquises:

'Shall I go out now to do the shopping or shall I wait till later?

'It's ten o'clock now and it's fine. The last three mornings it's started to rain at eleven. But everyone else will have noticed this and be going now, so the shops will be very crowded. And John might turn up later with the car and offer to take me, otherwise I shall have to walk. But if I wait till later all the best cabbages will have gone. If I go now I shall probably meet Mrs Smith and I don't want to do that—but come to think of it Mrs Smith won't be there because she's away on holiday, so I'd better go later. We were all specially asked to shop early this week to avoid the rush, so I'd better go now. Oh dear! What shall I do?'

This is obviously a very trivial bit of thinking and it may not lead us to think very highly of Mrs Jones's intelligence. But there is no doubt about the fact that it is practical and not artificial, it is in touch with experience, it is derived from things that actually happen.

It is obvious that neither we nor anyone else can solve Mrs Jones's problem for her. Unlike the previous questions we have considered there is no clearcut answer that follows necessarily from the data.

What Mrs Jones is trying to do is to decide on a course of action. She is making predictions about what the weather will be like, whether John will turn up, when the shops will be most crowded, whether the cabbages will be sold and so on. These predictions will be based on her previous experience and observations and what she has learned about the laws of cause and effect. Some of her predictions may turn out to be true, some false. Some will be made by her with conviction, some with hesitancy. She thinks that various things may happen, but she would say that some are more likely than others. There are considerable differences about how *certain* she feels concerning various future events. She will balance the probabilities, and she will balance the desirabilities. How much does it matter if the shops are crowded, or if she shops in the rain? She will, we hope, come to a decision. It might be said that the sensible thing for her to do will be to choose the course that she thinks is most likely to lead to the most desirable result, though this statement would be rather muddled and ambiguous. Shall she choose course X which she considers gives a good chance of leading to moderately desirable result P, or shall she prefer course Y which she considers gives a much smaller chance of leading to a far more desirable result Q? Which she does will depend largely on her temperament.

No certainty can result from this kind of thinking. It is a compound of predictions, tracing of cause and effect, balancing of probabilities and desirabilities. Not only can it produce no certainty as to the best course, but also when we look back afterwards we can usually only venture an opinion in a very limited way as to whether it was the best course. We can perhaps say whether Mrs Jones would have got wet if she had shopped at 11, instead of 10, but we can't be certain about that, somebody else might have come along and offered her a lift, she might have been run over.

It might be thought that this trivial piece of thinking on Mrs Jones's part is of a type that is not important. But if we reflect we see that not only is it of a type that we all undertake frequently in our personal daily lives, but also it is of the type that statesmen, industrialists, and all those who are responsible, individually and collectively, for the big and important decisions that deeply affect our lives, must be making the whole time. When statesmen wonder whether to declare war, when to hold a General Election, what their economic policy should be, whether to spend more money on the universities; when businessmen wonder whether to expand, whether to start manufacturing this new line, they are all undertaking a piece of thinking, based, as Mrs Jones's was, on a complicated compound of predictions, a tracing of causes and effects, a balancing of probabilities and desirabilities. The fact that it will now be a question of what is desirable not for a single individual but for a larger community, makes no difference to the shape and principles of the reasoning, though it may make a considerable difference to its importance.

Although, as we have pointed out, it is impossible to be certain what would have happened if the decisions had been different, nevertheless most people are convinced that some decisions made by our leaders in the past have been better (that is, have led to more desirable results) than others, and that some people habitually make better decisions than others. It seems reasonable to suppose that these better decisions are more likely to be made by people who understand and think clearly and who have studied the principles of the kind of thinking they are trying to do.

Let us look now at a slightly different type of open system thinking.

TROUBLE WITH THE KETTLE

The electrician comes along to find out why the kettle won't boil. This is clearly a much more cut-and-dried business than Mrs Jones and her shopping hours. Without going into technical details we can see the lines on which the electrician will think and act. He knows what causes or should cause the kettle to boil and he will try to find out which of these causes are lacking or defective. There is here, in a sense, a *right* answer to the problem: whatever will make the kettle boil now. But it might be misleading to say that there is a uniquely right answer. There could be slightly different ways of mending what was wrong, perhaps a makeshift method as opposed to a more permanent one. And his action may be affected by something else going wrong, another faulty connection, a power cut. His solution is not necessarily and uniquely right.

In order to be a good electrician he must understand clearly the chain of causes and effects in electrical systems, and it is probable that experience will be the most important factor in any success he may have.

SOME FURTHER EXAMPLES

We consider now rather more formally another example of open system reasoning.

'With a growing population and a rising standard of living the total number of cars on the roads since the war has inevitably risen steeply. Unfortunately owing to the neglect of successive Governments the total amount of road space has nowhere near increased in proportion. The congestion on our roads is already a serious impediment to our economic progress and general welfare and the prospects for the future, unless vigorous action is taken, are frightening indeed. What form should this vigorous action take?

'First we must have more and better roads. But at the same time it is essential that we should preserve what the mechanisation of the twentieth century has left to us of the amenities of our unrivalled countryside. It is neither possible nor desirable to have a road sys-

15

tem which will enable the whole population of London to go to Brighton, if they wish to, on a Sunday afternoon. Nor need we cater for all the inhabitants of the suburbs bringing their cars in to central London on the same day. We must see to it that fewer people want to do these things at any time. This can be done partly by stopping altogether the nonsense of Bank holidays and by spreading the load of holidays and leisure time more evenly; and partly by using much more the traditional weapon of higher prices to restrict demand when it exceeds supply. If too many people want to take their cars to Brighton at the same time, make it very expensive for them to do so. Increase steeply, especially at peak periods, the parking fees in London.'

First of all we have a statement of facts (large increase in number of cars, much smaller increase in road space), and of the causes which have produced those facts. The facts would probably not be disputed, and could easily be checked. There might be differences of opinion about the causes, some people might object for example to the word 'neglect'. We note how difficult it may be to distinguish between statements of opinion and of fact, and how easily the former may parade as the latter.

We then have the suggested consequences of these facts, the statement that they are undesirable and a question about possible remedies. Two things are then said to be desirable (better roads, preservation of amenities), but we are not told how the conflicting claims are to be reconciled. Two suggestions are then made of methods whereby the excessive demand for roads at certain times might be diminished.

This passage is not set down as an example of particularly good or bad reasoning in an open system, but merely to illustrate again the essential features: facts and opinion, suggested chains of cause and effect, predictions about the consequences of certain actions, a balancing of desirabilities and of probabilities. There is an obvious tendency when arguing a case to stress the possible desirable consequences of a suggested course of action and to neglect the undesirable ones. To the first suggestion in the passage above, for example, it might be objected that to spread leisure time more evenly in the week might mean many more people working on Sundays and a further infringement of the Sabbath; it might also be objected that it would make it more difficult for different members of a family to have their leisure at the same time. To the second suggestion it might be objected that this might involve unreasonable hardship to those for whom a car in London is a virtual necessity. Obviously these disadvantages must be balanced against the advantages.

A related tendency is shown in the following passage. It is a letter to *The Times* written in connection with the fact that a considerable number of British scientists were emigrating to go to academic and industrial jobs in America.

'Sir,
There cannot be much wrong with our own Higher Education if America with all her vast resources has to recruit scientists from our own meagre numbers.
Yours etc.'

It is clear that the writer's conclusion is much too sweeping and general. It would certainly be reasonable to deduce that we turn out some top class scientists, but we can make no inference about the standard of our Higher Education in other subjects, nor can we even say that the *general* standard of our Higher Education in science necessarily compares favourably with America. It might be that our educational methods are geared mainly to the production of the very best and that the less gifted are neglected. And is it fair to deduce from a comparison of our education with only one country that there is not much wrong with it? It might further be argued, though this is a point not covered by the letter, that whatever the quality of our Higher Education now, it is likely to be less good in the future if a lot of our best professors and lecturers go to America.

CERTAINTY

We all like to be certain, to know where we are, and it has been a natural tendency on the part of mankind to strive to find in the open system of his thinking about the world of experience the necessity or certainty that he finds in the closed system of the world of his own artificial construction. In Euclidean Geometry there is a set of axioms on which the thinking is based. If these axioms are accepted certain results necessarily follow. And the whole structure is one which can give considerable intellectual pleasure and satisfaction to those who have constructed it or understood it. Those whose minds have been trained on such systems have often tried to apply the same methods to the world of experience and have hoped and expected that they would thus be able to reach certain or necessary conclusions. These attempts, however—and there have been very many of them in the history of thought—are doomed to failure.[1] We shall have more to say about this later, but it may be worth making here in a preliminary way the simple, basic point that the necessity which we find in our closed systems of thinking is of our own making, *we* put it there by constructing the axioms, by not allowing any element of uncertainty to come in.

It might be objected that although the problem on p. 2 about Litt, Mitt and Nitt is obviously an artificial one, it need not be. They could be real people and real countries. The conclusion would then be just as necessary or certain, but the system, it might be claimed, would now be an open one. The answer to this would be that the solution is only a necessary one if the problem is insulated from the real world. Mitt must not be allowed to change his name; Nod must not be absorbed into Lod as the result of a sudden attack. The real world of events must be prevented from impinging.

In the open system exercises that follow the reader is on the whole being asked to consider arguments which are compounded of statements of fact, opinion, cause and effect, predictions and so on. There will be no necessary solutions though often the suggested criticisms will be such that we can feel that there is likely to be a general measure of agreement. As with the closed system exercises, we are going to consider the principles more formally and fully in later chapters. But it may be useful for the reader to exercise his critical faculties on them at this stage.

---

[1]As Sir Julian Huxley has said: 'To become truly adult we must learn to bear the burden of incertitude.' (*On Living in a Revolution*. Chatto & Windus.)

Exercises

1.17. Consider Mrs Jones's soliloquy on p. 12. Set out the points for and against her shopping now. From the evidence available what would be your advice to her and why?

1.18. 'If prices go up it will be to the advantage of the producers. for they will increase their profits; if prices go down it will be to the advantage of the consumers for they will pay less. The one thing that should definitely not happen therefore is that prices should remain as they are.' Discuss.

1.19. Comment on the following:
 'Women who smoke are more likely to give birth to girls than boys, says an American survey. Nonsense. I have never smoked and I have four girls and two boys. My eldest daughter smokes heavily and she has three boys and one girl.' (Letter to the *Daily Express*

1.20. 'The value to the community of a census is well established. The fact that the Government has authorised the expenditure of £3,000,000 is sufficient evidence of this.' (Letter to *Daily Express*) Discuss.

1.21. 'How disgraceful it is that in this day and age so large a proportion of our population is still getting less than the national average wage.' Do you agree?

1.22. 'It is remarkable that the most unhealthy countries, where there are the most destructive diseases, such as Egypt and Bengal, are the most populous.' (Boswell, *Life of Johnson*) Do you agree that it is remarkable?

1.23. Smith reads in the paper: 'More than half of those who have applied for tickets will be disappointed' and thinks 'Well, I suppose the unselfish thing to do would be for me to withdraw my application and make it more likely that someone else will be able to go.'

He then goes on to read: 'More than half of all people now alive will die before they are sixty', and thinks 'Well, I suppose the unselfish thing to do would be for me to die before I'm sixty, and make it more likely that someone else will live a bit longer.' Is he being rational? If not, explain clearly why not.

1.24. If you are told that a large number of A's are B's it is possible that being an A is the cause of being a B, that being a B is the cause of being an A, that being an A and being a B are both due to a common cause, or that as far as one knows there is no causal connection.

What do you think is the connection, if any, in the following cases?

1. Statistics show that over 90% of pipe smokers wear trousers.
2.   „   „   „   „   „ of jockeys are under 10 stone.
3.   „   „   „   „   „ of snail-eaters speak French.
4.   „   „   „   „   „ of bookmakers die before they are 90.

1.25. The following sentences appear to be of the same structure, but there is an important difference between the implied causal connections.

Explain this.

1. He touched nothing that he did not adorn!
2. He ate nothing that he did not like!

1.26. Discuss the argument of the following passages:

1. 'You want to give your aunt a lift to church in the car? But if you do that Bill and I will have to walk to the golf club; we'll keep our opponents waiting, and we'll probably miss our place in the queue. We may well be deprived of our game. Furthermore there are already quite enough cars outside St Mary's on Sunday mornings without adding to their number. How will making four men miss their golf and increasing the traffic congestion in the High Street help your aunt?'

2. 'A Glasgow shipyard hopes to win an order for a £500,000 dredger from South Africa.

'Few places in Britain need work more urgently than the Clyde, where unemployment is three times the national average.

'However, the search for business may be frustrated because in another Scottish town, Aberdeen, the council is boycotting South African goods as a protest against apartheid.

'The fear is that the South Africans will retaliate against Glasgow.

'Here is yet another demonstration of the utter futility of boycotts.

'How will making Scottish shipworkers idle help the coloured peoples of South Africa?' (*Daily Express*: Opinion)

1.27. Explain the following:

'Mr Langton having repeated the anecdote of Addison having distinguished between his powers in conversation and in writing, by saying 'I have only ninepence in my pocket; but I can draw for a thousand pounds.' *Johnson:* 'He had not that retort ready, Sir: he had prepared it beforehand.' *Langton* (turning to me): 'A fine surmise. Set a thief to catch a thief.' (Boswell, *Life of Johnson*)

1.28. 'Young people who want to buy their own homes face one great obstacle: the heavy deposits which many building societies expect them to find. Now chiefs of the societies' association are considering whether to give 100 per cent advances. Let them not hesitate. With advancing prices, there is no risk in lending money against the security of property.

'And there is certainly no risk in placing faith in the thriftiness of young people. Just look at the figures for savings. They are a record!' (From the *Daily Express*)

What are the reasons given for the two 'there is no risk...' statements? Do they seem to you to be adequate?

1.29. Discuss the argument of the following passages:
1. 'If you move to the South you go nearer the Equator, nearer the sun and warmth with all the accompanying benefits to health. If you move to the West property is cheaper, prices lower, life less hectic and rushed. If you move to the North you will find that the inhabitants have a more rugged charm, that the air is more bracing, more British. If you move to the East you will be nearer the great metropolis, the hub of the universe, the centre of decisions; you will

feel that you are more truly part of the life of the nation. Whichever way you move there are advantages. The one course for which there is no argument is to stay where you are.'

2. 'No matter which way the £'s value went there would be benefit for Britain. If its value fell there would be a quick corrective because British exports would immediately become cheaper and therefore would soar. If its value increased then each £ would buy more abroad, and thus the costs of imports would come tumbling down.' (*Daily Express*)

1.30. 'To say that if there were fewer foxhunters there would be fewer foxes is as true as to say that if there were fewer laws there would be fewer criminals.' (Letter to the *Sunday Times*)

Do you think it is 'as true'? Discuss.

Discuss also to what extent the connection between fewer foxhunters and fewer foxes is similar to that between fewer laws and fewer criminals.

1.31.-You go into the kitchen at 8.0 a.m. to prepare breakfast. You have to do last night's washing up (the same crockery is required), make tea and toast, boil eggs for three and lay the table. There is no hot water to be obtained from the tap, but you have an electric kettle, which takes 4 minutes to boil when full, and a medium-sized saucepan. You require one full kettle of boiling water for washing up and another for making the tea. The operation of washing up will take 7 minutes, and that of laying the table will take 4 minutes (of which 2 minutes only will be spent on laying last night's crockery). The amount of water required for boiling the eggs would take 4 minutes to boil in the saucepan or 2 minutes in the kettle. The three eggs are to be boiled for 3, 4 and 4½ minutes respectively.

Allowing 3 minutes for filling kettles, taking eggs out of saucepans, making tea, etc., what is the earliest time at which breakfast can be ready? Suggest what you think is the best order for the various operations.

If a helper is available what time will breakfast be ready? (Assume that with two people the times for washing up and laying the table will be halved.)

This exercise is a good example of the differences and connections between a closed and open system. At first sight, since it is clearly concerned with our daily living, it might appear to belong to an open system. But in real life there is scope for variation and interference; the telephone might ring; you might decide to wash up with water that is not quite boiling. Since you are required to assume that things like this do not happen, since nothing is allowed to go wrong, it becomes an artificial, closed system exercise and should be solved as such. The answers will therefore be exact. And of course provided the assumptions approximate to what happens in your real kitchen they may give a useful guide to the earliest time at which breakfast can be expected. The study of this and similar exercises with the assumptions of a closed system may help very much in the discovery of the most efficient and economical methods for tackling all sorts of practical problems.

SUMMARY

1. The main point of this chapter has been to make clear the distinction between closed and open system problems and to give some practice in tackling both kinds.

2. A closed system problem is one which is shut off from events in the real world. Various assumptions are fixed and given and conclusions follow from them necessarily. The *contingent*, by which we mean actual happenings, is not allowed to intervene.

3. An open system problem is a real world, contingent problem. It must usually be tackled by studying causes and effects and balancing probabilities and desirabilities. Conclusions will not be necessary, but more or less certain.

4. If open system problems are tackled with closed system methods, there is a danger that the thinking will be too rigid, insufficiently flexible, and that not enough allowance will be made for the uncertainties of real life.

5. But nevertheless it will often be useful in open system problems to make assumptions that are approximate, and to ignore the possibility of other events intervening. In such cases it will clearly be important to remember that the appearance of precision and certainty which such methods give may be misleading.

Chapter 2

Rules

In the first chapter we have had a preliminary canter. We have taken a look at some of the processes through which we go when we are thinking; we have tried our hand at some exercises and discovered to some extent how effectively our minds operate. In subsequent chapters we examine rather more closely and formally the most important and fundamental of these processes and the implements which we have at our disposal. In this chapter we consider and analyse rules of thought and of action, and the reasoning that is connected with applying, understanding, discovering, criticising and constructing them.

APPLYING A RULE

One of the very first steps that anyone takes in thinking is to apply a rule. Rules may be of very different kinds, but the essential thing they generally have in common is that they must be obeyed or applied or used for easier or more successful living, to avoid trouble or pain, to get the right answer. The rules that are pinned up on the school notice board must be obeyed in order to avoid punishment; unless we observe the rules of football the referee will blow his whistle; unless we can learn to apply correctly the rules for tying a tie we shall be objects of derision; if we fail to follow the rules or instructions for servicing the car it is likely to let us down; if we are unable or unwilling to apply the rules for multiplication we won't get our sums right. In some of these cases it might be thought more appropriate to use the word 'principles' or 'recommendations' rather than 'rules', but the word 'rules' can be applied if we remember that we are using it widely and loosely.

Most of these rules are quite clearly rules of action in an open system. The rule for multiplication might be called a rule of thought, though in a sense action is required as well. We need not

25

worry about trying to make the distinction between the two clear cut, but we note that in the early stages of our education, using the word in its widest sense, we are mainly occupied in collecting a large store of rules of all kinds and learning how to apply them. To start off with, the rules of action are often negative: 'Don't tread on the best carpet with muddy boots', 'Don't sit down unless there's something to sit on.' In order to comply with such instructions we need to recognize and remember rather than to use our reason. It is also the case that in the early stages the rules of thought, the rules we learn in the classroom, do not require very hard thinking.

It is in rules of thought that we are mainly interested now; let us look at some of them.

The rule for bringing pounds to grams is one which might be called a tight, rigid rule; there is no room for manoeuvre, and no possibility of differences of interpretation. It can perfectly well be followed blindly without having any idea what pounds or grams are. Similarly the rules for putting simple English sentences into Latin are tight and rigid. The general rules or principles for the formation of English sentences, however, are wider and looser; they have to be because there are so many different possibilities.

The more rigid and clearcut the rule is the easier it is to apply; it is therefore a natural and inevitable tendency for the early stages of many educational subjects to be reduced to clear, simple rules. It is an essential part of our education to learn to understand and apply such rules, sometimes blindly without having any idea of what we are doing or why. But it is much more important to be able to understand why the rules are as they are, if there is any reason.

Everyone who has studied mathematics knows the distinction between applying a rule or using a formula, perhaps blindly, and understanding the principle involved. It is sometimes a temptation for less able mathematicians and those who teach them, to concentrate on the mechanical application of a few simple rules, since in the short run this may make the passing of examinations more likely. But it will be essential for anyone who wants to master more advanced mathematics to understand what is happening, and it would I think be universally agreed that to understand is more educationally desirable than just to remember and carry out a mechanical process. It is more desirable because the person who understands is more likely to react appropriately to a difficult or unusual situation, and also more likely to enlarge the frontiers of our knowledge.

It is true that in some subjects there are rules for which no satisfying fundamental reason can be given. We have to learn the rules of syntax in a language, and we have to understand how they work. At the same time we may feel that they might just as well have been different in a way the principles of arithmetic could not have been.

Learning rules, applying them and, when possible, understanding them, are not in general enough. We must be prepared also to analyse them, to see what purpose, if any, they fulfil; and prepared also to be critical of both the objective and the method, perhaps in the hope of suggesting improvements. This applies to rules both of thought and of action.

Sometimes too we want to be able to deduce from events, or trains of thought, what the principles or rules are behind them. Finally, and this may be the most difficult thing of all, we want to be able to construct rules or principles for the solution of the intractable problem or the achievement of the difficult task.

In this book we are attempting to study some rules or principles of thinking. But from what we have just been saying it is obvious that it would not be very satisfactory merely to supply the reader with a set of formulae. We shall try to stress the importance of thinking that is based on thoroughly understood basic principles, but is flexible and adaptable. We must be able in all our thinking, as in mathematics, to apply wide principles to the variety of subjects that we are considering. What we must not do is to restrict our thinking to closed system problems for which rigid formulae can be devised and to which the answers are certain. We must try to devise a formula for using as few formulae as possible; we must be alertly, critically on our intellectual toes.

In the exercises at the end of this chapter, we provide opportunities for practising the application of routine and often silly and purposeless rules. (The merit of making them silly is to encourage the reader not to take rules for granted and suppose that they always have a sensible purpose, though of course they very often do.)

We also provide practice in deducing or spotting what the rule is. Many, indeed most, questions in Intelligence Tests are of this type and it may be helpful here to say something about the most profitable method of tackling them.

A very common type of question asks for the next term in a series. If we are asked for the next number after 3, 6, 9, it is easy to see that the rule is to add 3 and the next number is 12. Suppose however that we are asked for the next term after 4, 6, 9. We notice that 2 has been added the first time and 3 the second time, it seems reasonable to say therefore that 4 should be added the next time, making the fourth term 13. On the other hand we might also notice that 6 is $1\frac{1}{2}$ times 4 and 9 is $1\frac{1}{2}$ times 6. Perhaps therefore the rule is always to multiply by $1\frac{1}{2}$, which would make the fourth term $13\frac{1}{2}$. (The question might make it clear that the answer had to be a whole number in which case the latter solution would not be acceptable.) In order to make the rule clearer it would be advisable to give a greater number of terms. Even when this is done it may sometimes be possible to think of more than one rule that will produce the facts that are given, and there may be no way of judging between them; one answer may be just as 'good' or 'correct' as the other. On the whole, however, it is a sensible general principle to assume that the simpler rule is the one that is more likely to have been in the mind of the setter of the question.

Let us look now at some examples from Intelligence Tests.

'Insert the missing number.

$$4 \quad 9 \quad 17 \quad 35 \quad — \quad 139.'$$

(H. J. Eysenck, *Know your own I.Q.*)

We examine the differences between the terms, we examine their ratios, their comparative sizes. It is clear that the differences are increasing rapidly, and we notice that the second, third and fourth terms are each approximately double the preceding term and the sixth term is approximately four times the fourth term. It is a fairly easy step from this to see that a rule of alternately doubling and adding one, and doubling and subtracting one will fit the facts that we are given. The fifth term will therefore be *69*.

Let us consider another:

'Insert the missing number.

4	8	20
9	3	15
6	6	—'

(H. J. Eysenck, *Know your own I.Q.*)

It would be natural to look for differences or ratios across or down, but no pattern emerges here. We notice however that the numbers in the third column are bigger than any of the others, indeed bigger than the sum of the others. We may notice then that $4+(2\times8)=20$, and that $9+(2\times3)=15$. In other words a rule that produces 20 and 15 is to double the number in the second column and add it to the number in the first column. The missing number would therefore be *18*.

We might also notice, however, that, if we look down rather than across, the third number in both the first two columns is the result of adding 1 to the difference between the first two numbers. According-ing to this rule the answer would be 6.

There seems to me to be no good reason for preferring one of these answers to the other; they are both the results of rules neither of which seems to have a claim to be simpler or better. As I write this I do not know which is the answer in the book, but I would guess it to be 18, merely on the grounds that most of the rules seem to work across rather than down.

(I now look up the answer and see that it is given as *either* 24 *or* 18. I leave it as an exercise to the reader to discover by what rule 24 is obtained.)

It will be seen from this how difficult it is to ensure that there is only one answer, and certainly when there is more than one it is often not easy to see valid grounds for preferring one to others. Answers that are 'wrong', that is answers which do not follow from the rules that have been intended or thought of—for example the answer 6 in the last exercise—will presumably receive no marks, for the person tested will not normally have the opportunity to explain what his rule was. This does not seem very satisfactory.

We notice also that examples of this kind will obviously be very much easier with practice and experience of the sort of rules that are devised, in particular with experience of the workings of the mind of the particular person who is setting them.

To do them may be useful intellectual exercise, and we provide practice in this in the examples that follow, but too much impor-tance should not be attached to success or failure in this kind of thinking.

Exercises

2.1. The natives of the island of Hilary (Hilarians) fix their feast-day (Whupie) according to the following rule:

'Whupie shall be on that Saturday which is as many Saturdays after the first Saturday in February as the last digit in the year or the last digit but one in the year which ever is greater' (e.g. in 1977 it was 7 Saturdays after the first Saturday in February), 'unless it is a leap year in which case it shall be one Saturday later.'

When was Whupie in 1964? (1 March was a Sunday.) What was the last year in which Whupie was in February?

2.2. p, q, r . . . etc., stand for statements which can be true or false.

p → q   means that if p is true, q is true,
                and if p is false, q is false.

p ᙏ q   means that if p is true, q is false,
                and if p is false, q is true.

p ⌢ q   means that if p is true, q is true,
                and if p is false, q is true.

p ⌣ q   means that if p is true, q is false,
                and if p is false, q is false.

You are told that p is true and that

$$p → q ᙏ r ⌣ s ⌢ t ᙏ u → v ⌢ w ⌣ x.$$

Discover whether q, r, s, t, u, v, w, x are true or false.

2.3.   A ' perfect' word is one that starts with a vowel, a ' pluperfect' word is one that starts with two vowels; an 'imperfect' word is one that starts with a consonant.

To 'reform' a sentence is to arrange the words in order of perfection, first the pluperfect words, then the perfect, then the imperfect. The pluperfect and perfect words should be arranged among themselves in alphabetical order; the imperfect words should be arranged among themselves in reverse alphabetical order.

Reform the following sentences:

1. The slaves were threatened with spears and arrows by eight soldiers.
2. A reward of either a zebra or a washing machine was promised to each of the successful competitors.

3. My Aunt Eileen seemed to be ailing and I therefore asked the headmaster for leave to visit her.

2.4. The rules for quigglifying a number are as follows:
1. subtract from it the sum of its digits;
2. divide the result by 9;
3. subtract from the result the sum of all the digits of the original number except the last one;
4. divide the result by 10.

The result of this division is the quiggle of the original number.

Quigglify, or find the quiggles of, the following: 176; 4827; 85; 563; 7; 37621.

2.5. If you are told what the quiggle of a number is (see preceding question) is it possible to find with certainty what the original number was?

Find numbers which when quigglified become: (a) 83; (b) 7; (c) 17; (d) 122; (e) 245.

Are there some numbers which are not the quiggles of any number?

2.6. Find the missing numbers in the following and in each case explain the rule. (If you think there are possible alternatives say what they are and justify them):

(a)	7	6	19		(b)	9	14	20	
	5	8	21			8	11	16	
	4	11	—			13	7	—	
(c)	5	7	13		(d)	3	7	17	
	4	9	24			8	5	37	
	7	10	—			5	6	—	
(e)	3	6	15	39	—	(f)	2	8	5
						7	3	9	
						13	27	—	
(g)	3	10	29	88	—				

2.7. The attendance at the Utopia factory on any day except the opening day is determined entirely by who was there on the preceding day. There are 5 employees, A, B, C, D, and E, and the rules for attendance are as follows:

A will attend today if and only if B was present and C absent

yesterday

B	,,	,,	,,	C	,,	,,	D	,,
C	,,	,,	,,	D	,,	,,	E	,,
D	,,	,,	,,	E	,,	,,	A	,,
E	,,	,,	,,	A	,,	,,	B	,,

On the day the factory opened A, C and E were present. Write down the attendances for the next six days.

Who was present on the factory's 100th day, 383rd day?

2.8. As in the last question attendance at the Utopia factory on any day is to be determined entirely by who was there on the preceding day.

There are 5 employees, A, B, C, D, E. The managing director asks you to draw up the simplest set of rules that will ensure that after the attendance of C, D and E on the first day there shall always be 3 people present and that over each period of five days all employees attend equally often. What rules will you draw up?

2.9. The 'quare' of 273 is 278

,,	,,	192 ,, 188
,,	,,	576 ,, 583
,,	,,	671 ,, 663
,,	,,	891 ,, 900
,,	,,	112 ,, 115
,,	,,	401 ,, 395

Deduce the rule for finding the quare of a number of three figures.

Write down the quares of 712, 109, 472.

2.10. The 'igg' of 273 is 269

,,	,,	412 ,, 404
,,	,,	119 ,, 120
,,	,,	842 ,, 826
,,	,,	751 ,, 758
,,	,,	362 ,, 365

Deduce the rule for finding the igg of a number of three figures. Write down the iggs of 271, 442, 562, 973.

2.11. Find as many alternatives as you can for the missing numbers in the following. In each case explain the rule:

(a)	3	5	12		(b)	4	10	32
	4	7	24			5	7	27
	5	9	—			3	11	—
(c)	9	20	11		(d)	10	8	12
	11	17	12			13	17	24
	4	6	—			23	25	—

2.12. Investigate the possibility of finding a number of three figures whose igg is equal to its quare (see questions 2.9, 2.10).

2.13. The pseudonyms of JONES, SMITH and PERIWINKLE are respectively KNODT, TLJSI and QDSHXHOJMD.

What is the rule for finding pseudonyms? Write down the pseudonym of ROBINSON.

2.14. A notice goes up:

'All those who have not already drawn their subsistence allowance this week should report to the Deputy Assistant Bursar (D.A.B.) at 9 a.m. next Monday unless they failed to draw it last week in which case they shall be deemed to be without visible means of subsistence and should not report to anybody anywhere unless they are over 21 and/or have a maternal grandmother who is still alive in which case they should either report to the Substantive Acting Registrar at 10 p.m. on Tuesday or to the D.A.B. at 12 noon on Wednesday according to whether their surname begins with a letter in the first half of the alphabet or not unless their paternal grandmother has not got or did not have a British passport in which case they should report to the Warden as soon as possible unless they have already passed their driving test and/or have not got a bicycle in which case they should take a couple of aspirins and go quietly home to bed.'

Jones, aged 20, has not drawn his subsistence allowance this week or last. He has a bicycle but has not passed his driving test. Both his grandmothers are still alive and have British passports. What should he do?

2.15

p, q, r are three typical consecutive letters of the alphabet. You are told that:

if p ticks and q ticks, then r tocks;
if p ticks and q tocks, then r ticks;
if p tocks and q ticks, then r ticks;
if p tocks and q tocks, then r tocks.

1. What can you say about m if a ticks and b tocks?
2. What can you say about a if i ticks and j tocks?
3. What can you say about y if x tocks and z ticks?
4. If l ticks and p tocks, what can you say about m, n and o?

2.16. The high priests of the tribe of Temme have discovered by long experience that prayers are only acceptable to their gods if they are first refined by mogrification. There are two stages in this process: first, transmogrification which a low priest is qualified to perform, and secondly supermogrification which can only be undertaken by the highest of the high, the Arch Priest.

The rules for the transmogrification of a sentence are as follows:
1. The longest word shall have its vowels removed and placed in the same order after the first word (thus forming the second word): its consonants shall be reversed and placed at the end of the sentence.

(N.B. No sentence is mogrifiable unless it has a longest word which is not also the last word.)
2. The word that first was last shall have its consonants reversed and these shall be followed by its vowels in the original order. It shall then be placed where the longest word originally was.
3. The words that now are third and fourth shall be wedded the one to the other, and the result of this union shall be precisely bisected. The first half shall then be reversed and placed at the beginning; the second half shall be placed at the end.

For supermogrification there is one rule only:
Words that the fingers of the priest have hitherto left untouched shall be reverse-wedded in pairs, the first with the last, the second with the last but one and so on. (If there is an odd number of hitherto untouched words the middle one shall be reversed and left in the same position.) The result of each reverse-wedding shall be

precisely bisected and the first half shall be placed where the second member of the union was originally, while the second half shall be placed where the first member of the union was.

A recently discovered fully mogrified sentence ran as follows:

VNRUAOHB VEASNTK UAIO IMENE SKCRTI FO ASNED RHESQIU NTRTSRF TEISFTUL.

What was the original sentence? What are the rules for the wedding and reverse-wedding of words?

SUMMARY

1. Following rules of thought and of action is the basis of much of our reasoning and behaviour.

2. Rules may be rigid, tight principles which do not allow much room for manoeuvre, or they may be wider, looser principles.

3. It is important, not only to be able to follow them, but also to understand why they are as they are, if there is a reason. A blind following of rules, though sometimes useful, is often not educationally desirable.

4. It is important also to be prepared to be critical of rules; both of their objectives and methods.

5. For our thinking to be effective we must be able to follow and to understand rules, but it is important also to be flexible, adaptable, and to be able to apply wide principles.

6. We often want to be able to deduce from events or trains of thought the rules or principles that lie behind them. Practice in spotting the rule is provided by Intelligence Test types of question. It is useful to be able to do this, but it is only one kind of thinking.

Chapter 3

Classifications

A process that is a basic preliminary to much of our thinking, whether in a closed or an open system, is that of classifying, of placing objects or ideas in different categories, perhaps literally into different boxes or files. Unless our attention is called to it we may be hardly aware of the extent to which we do it and to which it is often taken for granted or assumed in our thinking.

A closer examination of what is happening, of the principles according to which it should be carried out, will help to clarify our reasoning in several important respects.

Many of the points that are going to be made in this chapter can be explained more clearly with the help of diagrams. Some people tend to react rather sharply against these and to associate them with what is difficult and complicated. I would assure anyone who feels like this that if he takes the following pages slowly and carefully each step really is very simple, and to understand these diagrams, to gain the mastery over them, and to feel that they are allies and not foes, will be a useful and important gain.

We start with a particularly simple idea on a very simple diagram:

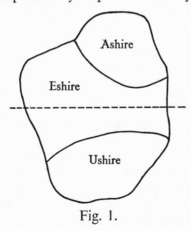

Fig. 1.

The figure represents the imaginary island of Then. It is divided into three counties, as shown, which are called Ashire, Eshire and Ushire. The inhabitants of these counties are called A's, E's and U's respectively. The island lies on the equator, represented in the diagram by a dotted line. The areas North and South of the equator are called Northen and Southen and their inhabitants Northeners and Southeners (N's and S's for short). It will be seen that every inhabitant of the island is either an N or an S, and is also either an A, or an E or a U.

Exercise 3.1

In the following sentences consider which of the three words 'all', 'some'or 'no' you would insert at the beginning.

1. A's are N's
2. U's are E's
3. S's are U's
4. N's are E's
5. N's are S's
6. U's are S's
7. E's are S's

We frequently use sentences which are of the same basic structure as the above to say that some, all or no A's are B's.

For example:

(a) Some bishops are Conservatives.
(b) All numbers ending in 6 are divisible by 2.
(c) No members of the House of Commons are clergymen.

The sentences concerning the inhabitants of the island of Then were about the areas in which they lived and could be understood easily by looking at the map. But (a), (b) and (c) cannot be deduced from any map and do not refer to positions in space. Nevertheless it will often be convenient to represent such statements by diagrams, and our thinking about them may thus be made simpler when we want to combine facts expressed by several interlocking statements. (All A's are B's; Some B's are C's . . . etc.)

The sentence (a) above might be represented thus:

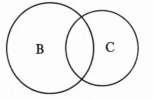

Fig. 2

where B represents bishops and C Conservatives. This would not at all imply that bishops and Conservatives are collected together in two overlapping areas, like Northern and Eshire on the map; but the diagram represents in a convenient pictorial form the state of affairs in which some bishops are Conservatives and some are not, and some Conservatives are bishops and some are not.

It is important to notice that the statement 'some B's are C's' might also be represented thus:

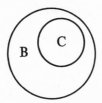

Fig. 3

In fact from our knowledge of bishops and the Conservative party in Britain we do not think that this would represent the true state of affairs; there are many Conservatives who are not bishops. Our experience leads us to suppose that the earlier diagram does represent the truth, as long as it is understood that the size of the circles or of the overlapping area is not intended to bear any relation to the numbers of people concerned.

Let us consider the next sentence, (b): 'All numbers ending in 6 are divisible by 2.' This might be represented in a diagram thus:

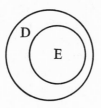

Fig. 4

where E stands for 'numbers ending in 6', and D for 'numbers divisible by 2'.

Notice however that the statement 'all E's are D's' might also be represented thus:

Fig. 5

with the two areas coinciding.

From our knowledge of arithmetic we know that Fig. 4 represents the true state of affairs, for there are a great many numbers which are divisible by 2 but do not end in 6.

The sentence (c), 'No members of the House of Commons are clergymen', can be represented thus:

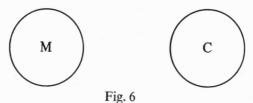

Fig. 6

where M and C stand for 'members of the House of Commons' and 'clergymen' respectively. Notice that there is no other way of representing the statement 'No M's are C's'.

THE IDEA OF A 'CLASS' OR 'SET'

In this chapter we have been using the idea of a class or set of people or things.

An obvious and easy example is the actual class or set of which anyone who is at school is a member at any time. And we all know that it is possible to be a member of one set for French and of a quite different set for Mathematics. Bishops, clergymen, Conservatives, members of the House of Commons, numbers ending in 6, are all classes. In some cases it is quite clear who or what the members of the class are, they are easily identifiable and there is a definite, perhaps quite small, number of them. This is true of members of the House of Commons at any moment. It is much less clear however who are members of the class 'Conservatives'. Are we referring only to this country? Do we mean those who would vote conservative if there were a general election today? It is obviously possible in theory to define the qualifications for membership of this class in such a way as to make it quite certain who does and who does not belong, but it might not be very easy in practice to produce a definition which would satisfy those who were interested. Generally we use the word in rather a loose, vague way and for most purposes it does not matter at all that this is so, though it may be very important indeed to recognise the fact in this and similar cases. We shall return to this point later.

It would be fairly easy to define 'bishops' and 'clergymen' in such a way as to make the classes clearcut. But we have got to agree about which countries and which churches are to be included.

With the classes of numbers ending in 6 or numbers divisible by 2 there will never be any doubt as to whether a particular number belongs. A distinctive feature of these classes, however, is that they each have an indefinitely large number of members. It might be objected that for this reason it is misleading to use closed circles to represent them as we have done in Figures 4 and 5. A diagram with the circles uncompleted would better represent the facts of the case. Thus:

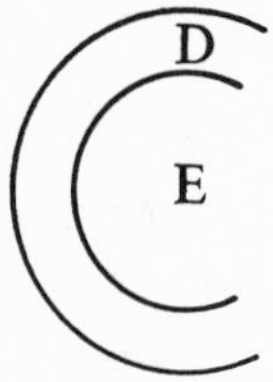

Fig. 7

It is worth noticing that these classes belong to a closed system, their membership is necessary, unchanging; whereas the classes of Conservatives, Bishops, etc., belong to an open system, their membership is sometimes uncertain, always subject to fluctuation.

'SOME'

It has probably already occurred to readers that the word 'some' is loose and vague. If I say that some of the apples on that tree look small I would almost certainly mean at least two but not all. 'Some' is generally used to imply 'at least two', but there may not be the intention to exclude the meaning 'all'. If a man is asked, for example, whether people in the village are satisfied with their new member of Parliament he might reply cautiously, 'Well, I know some of them are.' In such a context he would be likely to mean 'at least some': he has, perhaps, only heard the opinion of a few people; it is possible that all of them are, but he doesn't know. The vagueness of 'some' could often be lessened if one qualified it by saying 'only some' (and therefore not all) or 'at least some' (and therefore possibly all).

Suppose one is asked to represent by diagrams the statement 'at least some A's are not B's', where it is assumed that A's and B's stand for clearcut classes with definite numbers of members, so that they can be represented by circles as in preceding diagrams.

It is possible that all A's are not B's, in which case the diagram would look like this:

Or it is possible that some A's are not B's and some are B's, in which case the diagram could look either like this:

or like this:

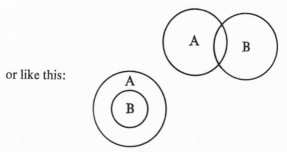

The reader should satisfy himself that there is no other possibility.

Exercises

3.2. Represent by diagrams the following statements, giving in each case all the possibilities:

1. Only some A's are B's.
2. All B's are A's.
3. At least some A's are B's.
4. Not all A's are B's.
5. Only some B's are not A's.
6. No A's are B's.

It will by now be clear that if there are two clearcut classes of A's and B's, for example present members of Greater Larning Grammar School and present members of Little Larning Cycling Club, the possible relationships between their members can be represented by the following diagrams:

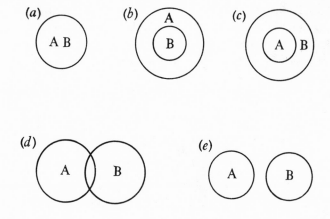

These five diagrams exhaust all the possibilities.

3.3. Describe in words, as briefly as possible, the situations represented by each of the above diagrams.

3.4. Draw diagrams to show the likely relationships between the following classes of members of a school (or preferably, if possible, the actual relationships, in your school).

1. The top science division; the school Rugby XV; the top history division.

2. Those who do French; those who do Mathematics; the school orchestra.

3. Those who do Chemistry; those who do History and Chemistry; those who are over 16.

4. Those who have had their birthdays this year; chess players; chess players under 14.

5. Those who smoke; those who have been to the cinema this week; those who play the piano.

Many people find that diagrams such as the above help to clarify their thinking about classes that are clearly defined. They are especially likely to be useful in bringing together several pieces of information about the same classes.

Suppose that you are told that all B's are A's, but not all A's are B's, and that only some C's are not B's. You are asked what can be said about A's and C's.

'All B's are A's, but not all A's are B's' can be represented thus:

and in no other way.

'Only some C's are not B's' can be represented either thus:

or thus:

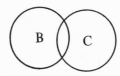

It will be seen that if these diagrams are combined the C circle might be drawn either so as to include the A circle, or to be entirely inside it or to overlap it. The conclusion therefore is that at least some C's are A's.

Consider another example:

'Only some A's are B's; at least some B's are not C's. What can you say about A's and C's?'

'Only some A's are B's' can be represented either thus:

or thus:

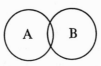

'At least some B's are not C's' can be represented either thus:

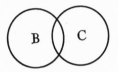

or thus:

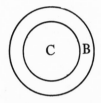

or thus:

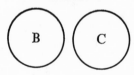

It will be seen that from this information the C circle might be drawn relative to the A circle in any one of the five ways that exhaust all the possibilities. Nothing therefore can be said about A's and C's.

In the following exercises your answers should be illustrated and supported by diagrams. Assume in each case that the classes are clearcut and contain a definite number of members.

Exercises

3.5. All A's are B's; all B's are C's. What can you say about A's and C's?

3.6. All A's are B's; all C's are B's. What can you say about A's and C's?

3.7. Only some A's are B's; some B's are not A's; all C's are A's. What can you say about B's and C's?

3.8. All those who shop at the Bonkshire Co-operative Stores live in the city of Bonk. Every single member of the Bonkshire Choral Society also lives in Bonk. Since Mrs Jones is a member of the Bonkshire Choral Society therefore she is among those who shop at the Bonkshire Co-operative Stores. Do you agree? Explain why, or why not.

3.9. Only some of those who watched Chelsea play football last Saturday watched them today. Most of those who watched them last Saturday and most of those who watched them today bought programmes. Binks watched them on both occasions, so he must certainly have bought at least one programme. Do you agree? Explain.

3.10. Only some of those who play tennis in Then also play cricket, but there is no one who plays cricket there who does not also play tennis. Only some of those who play cricket went to Spain for their holiday last year. Can you say whether any of the tennis players went to Spain?

MORE ABOUT CLASSES

In the exercises and examples which we have so far considered we have either called the classes A's, B's etc., and stated that they were clearcut, or considered classes such as 'those who watched Chelsea play football last Saturday' to which it would seem reasonable to say that any individual person either does or does not belong. We made this assumption because we were practising the handling, with the aid of clearly defined diagrams, of such statements as 'At least some A's are B's' etc.

We will now examine rather more closely the assumption about

47

clearcut classes and see what relation it bears to the facts of life.

Classes of things or people are collections which have something in common, which are like each other in certain ways. These common characteristics may be natural, they may be acquired, or they may be artificially imposed. It is also possible for them to be some combination of these.

The characteristics which cows have in common are natural, and however much we may want to it is not possible for us, or for monkeys or wasps, to acquire them, or at any rate to acquire all of them. Similarly the characteristics of being mountains over 10,000 feet or islands less than a certain size are natural.

The characteristic of having a golf handicap of less than 5 is acquired, as is the characteristic of having climbed Mount Everest or of being kind to old ladies.

It might be said however that the characteristic of being a member of the Lower IVth at Upper Larning Grammar School is artificially imposed, though there will certainly be good reasons why the membership is as it is.

Membership of the set of those who have played cricket for England will be partly the result of natural characteristics (the ability must have been there), partly of acquired (the ability had to be developed) and partly of artificial (there had to *be* an England and X had to be selected rather than Y).

In fact the classification of our characteristics is inevitably not a very clearcut one.

But whatever the nature and the origin of the common characteristics it is important to realise that they are very numerous and that it is *we*, individuals or collections of individuals, who decide which ones to select as a basis of our classifications.

Suppose a man has a large number of books, and he is arranging them in different shelves. It is possible that they might just be placed in the order in which they come to hand, with no particular principle in mind. It is more likely, however, that they will be classified in some way. They might be arranged according to their subject matter, with books on astronomy, bee-keeping and cookery in different shelves. This is the usual practice in libraries and is probably the most convenient for the student of various subjects. They might be arranged according to their colour; this is often done when the owners of the books are interested in aesthetic considerations and keep them as decorations rather than for reading. They might be arranged according to their heights: this classification could easily be dictated by variations in the sizes of the shelves. They might be arranged in alphabetical order of titles or of authors.

Normally those who classify or arrange the books will be doing so for a definite purpose; they pick out for their classification those characteristics or criteria which will result in the most convenient or pleasing arrangement. But it is important to notice that there is a very large number of other ways in which the books might have been classified. They might have been arranged according to the number of pages, their weight, their publishers, when or where they were acquired, how often they have been read. These characteristics and many others are no less real, though they may be less useful and interesting.

Some of these classifications are quite clearcut or can easily be made so. If we are arranging books in shelves according to whether they have less than 100 pages, from 100 to 200 pages and so on, there should never be any doubt as to where a book should go, provided we have agreed what to do about counting the fly-leaf, the index, the table of contents.

But if we are arranging them according to their subject matter it may be very difficult indeed, as anyone who has done it knows, to make the classification clearcut. Does a book on the philosophy of science go in the philosophy or in the science section? There is no right answer to this question; it is merely a matter of which is more convenient. If we classify them by weight (1 lb or less, between 1 lb and 2 lb. etc.) there need be no doubt as to the pile on which any given book is to be placed. But we note that the decision as to where the lines are to be drawn is bound to be somewhat arbitrary.

Man classifies for convenience and interest. Sometimes the dividing lines between the different classes are obvious and clearcut—as for example 2-wheeled, 3-wheeled and 4-wheeled vehicles. Sometimes, as when one is considering weights or lengths, there is an indefinitely large number of gradations between the lighter and the heavier, or the shorter and the longer. In such cases there are no natural or obvious dividing lines and though it is perfectly possible to make the divisions clearcut there is often an inevitable arbitrariness about just how it is done. Sometimes our classification is inevitably vague and to some extent a matter of opinion. Not only are the dividing lines not naturally clearcut but it is very difficult to make them so. This difficulty, as we have seen, arises obviously when we are classifying books by their subject matter. Ideally we want to agree on definitions which shall be roughly in accordance with general usage and which will enable us to decide unerringly into which section any book shall go. But this agreement will not be easy. It is of course bound up with the whole question of how words are used or defined and we shall have much to say about this later.

Similarly it would be very difficult to agree about the membership of the class of those who are kind to old ladies. Exactly what are we going to mean by 'kind'? How kind do they have to be? And how often? How old do the ladies have to be? I hope that readers are thinking that to make a clearcut class of this sort would be a very silly thing to want to do, and unlikely to fulfil any useful purpose.

Exercise 3.11

Do you think the following classes are clearcut or can easily be made so by a suitable definition? If the latter, suggest a definition. (Consider in each case how you would decide whether to admit a candidate for membership.)

1. Positive odd numbers less than 1,000
2. Clever men
3. Books about motor racing
4. Members of the Athenaeum (A club in London)
5. Wooden objects
6. Pictures
7. Chairs
8. Natural characteristics (see p. 46)
9. Wasps
10. Manual workers
11. The aristocracy
12. Saints
13. Antique furniture
14. Bungalows
15. Left-handed Frenchmen

'EXCLUSIVE' AND 'EXHAUSTIVE' CLASSIFICATIONS

To some extent we have already considered by implication whether various classifications are exclusive or exhaustive. Classifications are exclusive if there is no overlap, no members common to the different sets. The classes, for example, of those who voted Conservative, those who voted Labour, and those who voted Liberal in the last election in this country are exclusive. The classes of bankers and Conservatives are not. It will often be the case that even when classes are not clearcut we can say without hesitation that they are or are not exclusive. The classes of gardeners and of Liberals, for example, are not usually very clearly defined, but even if we leave the definition vague we can agree that there are likely to be many people who are members of both. The classes of babies and the senile on the other hand, though far from clearcut are certainly exclusive.

Classifications are said to be exhaustive if they together include all the objects, people, etc., to which it is relevant to apply these classifications in the context under consideration. This definition is obviously somewhat loose, and perhaps not very clear. Examples may help. If we are talking about the classes of people under 20 and people over 50, it is likely that the totality in which we are interested is that of all people. These classes would therefore not be exhaustive. The classes of people under 40 and those over 30, however, would be exhaustive, though they would not be exclusive. There is no one who belongs to neither of these classes but some people belong to both.

A phrase that is sometimes used for the totality of things in which we are interested for particular classifications is 'the universe of discourse'. Other possible phrases are 'the field of reference' or 'the area of applicability'. (None of these seems entirely satisfactory. Perhaps the reader will be able to think of a better one.)

What the universe of discourse covers might seem in general rather hard to decide, in particular cases, however, it is usually as clear as one wants it to be. Whether it is necessary or desirable to define it precisely or nearly precisely depends on the purposes for which the classifications are being made. We return to this point below.

Exclusive and exhaustive classifications may usefully be represented in diagrams. These will be no harder to understand than those we have considered hitherto, but since they will be slightly more complicated it will be clearer to use rectangles and straight lines instead of circles.

In the following diagrams the outer rectangle represents in each case the whole universe of discourse or area of applicability.

If two classes A and B are exclusive but not exhaustive the situation is represented thus:

There is here an area in the middle which is neither A nor B.

If the two classes are exhaustive but not exclusive the situation is thus:

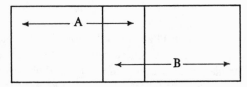

There is here an area which is both A and B.

If the two classes are neither exclusive nor exhaustive the situation is thus:

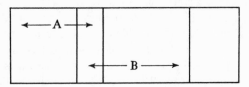

There is here an area which is both A and B and also an area which is neither.

If the two classes are both exclusive and exhaustive the situation is thus:

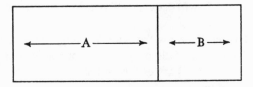

There is here no area which is both A and B or which is neither.

Similar diagrams could be constructed if there are 3 or more classes and their mutual exclusiveness and exhaustiveness are defined.

Exercises

3.12. Draw diagrams to represent the following situations:
1. A and B are exhaustive but not exclusive. B and C are exclusive but not exhaustive. (What can you say about A and C?)
2. B and C are neither exhaustive nor exclusive. A and C are exclusive and exhaustive. (What can you say about A and B?)
3. A, B and C are mutually exclusive but together not exhaustive.

3.13. A and B are exclusive and exhaustive. B and C are exclusive. Can you deduce whether A and C are exclusive or exhaustive?

3.14. B and C are neither exclusive nor exhaustive. A and B are exclusive. Can you say whether A and C are exclusive or exhaustive?

3.15. Consider whether the following classes are (a) exclusive, (b) exhaustive. (Discuss any difficulties you think there might be about defining the universe of discourse.)
1. E's and U's (see diagram on p. 36)
2. N's and A's (see pp. 36, 37)
3. Equilateral triangles; Isosceles triangles
4. Odd numbers; multiples of 4
5. 8-sided figures; 10-sided figures
6. Bungalows; houses
7. Florins; shillings
8. Those who have studied English at school; those who have studied French at school
9. Bishops; members of the M.C.C.

THE PURPOSES OF CLASSIFICATION

Whether classifications are exhaustive depends, as we have seen, on the definition of the universe of discourse, which in turn depends on the context and the purposes for which the classification is being carried out. It is very important indeed to remember that classification is not in general a sensible end in itself. To put marbles actually or in imagination into different bags according to their colour, size, weight, country of origin, is merely a playing with marbles unless it fulfils some useful purpose.

Let us consider, therefore, for what sort of purpose, if any, some of the classifications considered in *3.11* might be useful or interesting, and also—and this is an extremely important point—whether it is likely to matter for the purposes for which we are going to use the classifications if they are precise or not.

Some of them—positive odd numbers less than 1,000, wasps—are clearcut and precise; they call attention to obvious similarities to and differences from other numbers and animals that are important and significant not only to mathematicians and biologists, but also to individuals in their daily lives. If we are in charge of a demolition squad with instructions to pull down the odd-numbered houses, it is important for us to be able to recognise members of this class, and we can easily be taught to do so. If we are warned that wasps sting and should therefore be handled with care, it is important for us to be able to tell whether an animal is a member of 'Wasps', and again it is easy for us to learn to do this.

It is important that members of the Athenaeum shall be clearly defined, as they in fact are. The secretary is thus enabled to see to it that those who are members pay their subscriptions, and that those who are not do not enter the premises unless introduced by someone who is.

If we are asked to fetch a chair from the next room we want to be able to recognise members of this class, but we do not in general need to be too fussy and precise. It would be important to know what it was wanted for, and it would probably be wise to prefer this small, strong, low table which could clearly be used for sitting on, to that decayed object which certainly used to be a chair once, but from which one leg and the back have fallen off.

'Manual workers' is an interesting one. For ordinary conversational purposes most people would probably not be too fussy about membership. Is a lorry driver a member? Is a chauffeur? Does it matter? But there used to be a time when manual workers were not allowed to row at Henley Regatta. For that purpose, therefore, a clearcut definition was necessary.

The 'natural characteristics' that were referred to on p. 46 were distinguished from acquired and artificial characteristics. We pointed out then that the distinction was not entirely clearcut. It seemed useful and possibly helpful, however, to draw attention to certain distinctive features about the characteristics we were examining. It often helps us in our thinking to arrange things in an orderly manner, to classify, but it will often be foolish and wasteful of time and energy to attach a great deal of importance to the question of the compartment into which a borderline case should go. Sometimes it matters and then we have got to come to a decision. Very often it doesn't. We must try to bear in mind every time what we are doing the classification for.

The reader may now like to think for himself about the possible purposes of some of the other classifications in *3.11*.

THE USES AND LIMITATIONS OF DIAGRAMS

It is fairly obvious that in drawing a continuous line round an area to represent a class we assume a clearcut division or definition. When this represents or very nearly represents the true state of affairs, diagrams may be helpful.

If I am told that at least some of the under-16 inhabitants of Epsom passed through Piccadilly Circus last year, that nobody under 16 who passed through Piccadilly Circus last year had ever been to Timbuctoo, that at least some of the members of X Comprehensive School live in Epsom, and asked whether it is possible that Barbara Black aged 15, a member of X Comprehensive School, has ever been to Timbuctoo, I personally would find it helpful to set the facts out in diagrammatic form.

It might very reasonably be argued that such problems are not likely to be met with outside a book on 'thinking', but it could still be maintained that the doing of them could provide useful mental exercise if not indulged in to excess.

Very often in real life the classes are not clearcut and the thinking we are asked to do cannot be conveniently or accurately represented in terms of classes. In such cases it may be very misleading indeed to use diagrams.

Consider, for example, the following argument:

'No sensible man would forget to take his latchkey out with him. Anybody who has an insurance policy for his old age is certainly sensible. John Jones has got an insurance policy and therefore he cannot have forgotten his latchkey.'

It requires no formal study of thinking or of logic to see that this argument is absurd; though there is indeed a danger that those who have been introduced to such a study may say that 'logically' the argument is perfectly all right. It is such utterances that give logic a bad name.

If one were to take 'sensible people' as a clearcut class, represented by a circle, it would be easy to show in a diagram that the conclusion 'follows'. It should be obvious, however, that to do this would seriously misrepresent the facts. The word 'sensible' is used loosely, and whether we apply it to a person or action is to some extent a matter of opinion. We all of us do many things that we and others would describe as foolish (assuming that this is the opposite of sensible), but most of us also do things from time to time that would be agreed to be sensible. We can think of some people who very rarely do foolish things, and we might describe them as very sensible. It is sensible to have an insurance policy and foolish to forget one's latchkey. If John Jones has a reputation for doing sensible things, we should be surprised at his forgetting his latchkey, and we might search for reasons why he did it—for example that the alarm clock failed to go off that morning and he was in a hurry—but the logical argument is clearly ridiculous.

Exercise 3.16

In the following pieces of argument consider:

(a) whether diagrams are applicable,

(b) whether the conclusion follows as stated, and if it does not,

(c) what conclusion, if any, does follow.

1. Only some members of the Crumshire County Club are members of the town band. All my colleagues at the Bank belong to the Crumshire County Club and some of them do not live in Kruss. No one who lives in Kruss belongs to the town band. Therefore Browne, who is a colleague of mine at the Bank, cannot possibly be a member of the town band.

2. No intelligent person is in favour of our entry into the Common Market. Some people who are in favour of our entry into the Common Market are Liberals. Jones got a first class degree at the University and is one of the most intelligent men I know. Therefore he cannot be a Liberal.

3. All wise people are happy. Some happy people are not good-looking. Many good-looking people are not kind. Every kind person

is eminently lovable. It follows therefore that to be wise is to be lovable.

SUMMARY
1. We find people or things in separate or overlapping areas which can be represented by diagrams. Diagrams of this kind may be useful in helping us to think about groups or classes which have something in common.
2. If the classes are clearcut, the possible relationships between the members of two classes are shown on p. 42.
3. We consider some of the different ways in which, and purposes for which, people classify. We see that a great deal of the classification is very far from clearcut.
4. Two or more classifications may be *exclusive* or *exhaustive* or both or neither. These ideas are explained by diagrams on p. 50.
5. Whether it matters if classifications are or are not clearcut depends very much on the purposes for which they are being made. Some of these purposes are examined more closely.
6. It is important to realise that diagrams only apply to clearcut classes. To use them in arguments where the divisions between classes are not clear, or where the idea of classification is hardly applicable (e.g. the class of 'sensible people'), may be very misleading.

Chapter 4

Contradictories and Contraries

Suppose that we are sorting marbles and our instructions are to put every marble into one of two boxes, marked respectively 'White' and 'non-White'. Assuming that we have agreed upon a clear and precise definition as to what counts as white there would be no difficulty about this. For every marble we have to make a judgment: 'This is white', or 'This is non-white'; there is no other alternative. The two classifications are both exclusive and exhaustive.

These two statements: 'This is white' and 'This is non-white' are said to be *contradictory*. They cannot both be true, no marble can qualify for admission to both boxes; and they cannot both be false, every marble must qualify for admission to one or the other.

It might be thought that we all know what it is to contradict and that no formal explanation is necessary. The word 'contradictory', however, is used in logic in a way that is different in an important respect from that in which it is used in everyday speech. If I say: 'This marble is white' and you say 'It is red' you would normally be said to have contradicted me. In logic, however, that would be called not the contradictory, but a contrary.

CONTRARY

Suppose now that the two boxes which the marble-sorters have in front of them are marked 'white' and 'red'. The judgments which can be made are not only 'This is white', or 'This is red', there is also another alternative: 'This is neither.' The two classifications in this case, though they are still exclusive, are not now exhaustive.

These two statements: 'This is white' and 'This is red' are said to be contrary. They cannot both be true; no marble can qualify for admission to both boxes. But they *can* both be false; many marbles may qualify for admission to neither.

As we have pointed out, two statements which are contradictory

59

exhaust all the possibilities, but two statements which are contrary do not. It follows therefore from this that to every statement there is one and only one contradictory—the statement that comprises all the other possibilities. And it will simply take the form of a flat denial: the contradictory of 'A is B' is 'A is not B', though contradictories may sometimes be wrapped up in different language.

But a statement may have any number of contraries. We have seen that 'This marble is white' has as a contrary 'This marble is red' but there are also obviously a large number of other contraries: 'This marble is blue, green, yellow ... etc.'

It may be useful to repeat the formal definitions:

Two statements are contradictory if they cannot both be true together, and cannot both be false together.

Two statements are contrary if they cannot both be true together, but can both be false together.

It may not always be obvious whether two statements are contradictory, contrary or neither. Sometimes the use of diagrams may help. Consider, for example, the statements:

     (a) At least some A's are B's.   (b) No A's are B's.

(a) may be represented thus:

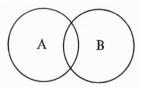

or thus:

or thus:

or thus:

(b) can only be represented thus:

Therefore they cannot possibly both be true together; and since between them they exhaust all the possible relationships between A's and B's they cannot both be false together.

They are therefore contradictories.

Consider another example:

(a) All A's are B's.   (b) Only some B's are not A's.

(a) may be represented thus:

or thus: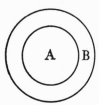

(b) may be represented thus:

or thus: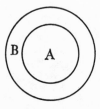

In this case if 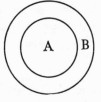 represented the actual state of affairs both the statements would be true. And since they can both be true together they are neither contradictories nor contraries.

Exercise 4.1

Consider whether the following pairs of statements are contradictory, contrary, or neither. (Assume that any classes referred to are clearcut.)

1. (a) This marble is white.   (b) This marble is not quite spherical.
2. (a) Tom is under 16.   (b) Tom is over 16.
3. (a) He was off-side.   (b) He was on-side.
4. (a) 'Methinks he doth protest too much.'   (b) He never utters.
5. (a) 'To be or   (b) not to be.'
6. (a) All members of the club under 30 were present.   (b) All members of the club over 30 were absent.
7. (a) Only some members of the cricket eleven are in the school orchestra.   (b) At least some members of the school orchestra are in the cricket eleven.
8. (a) That was a very brave thing to do.   (b) That was a very silly thing to do.
9. (a) Only some A's are B's.   (b) No B's are A's.
10. (a) All members of the Stock Exchange have incomes of £X a year, or over.   (b) At least some people with incomes under £X a year are members of the Stock Exchange.

More examples of contradictories and contraries

From what has already been said it will be obvious that in talking about contradictories we inevitably assume the existence of clearcut classes. And we have pointed out that this assumption is very often not legitimate. It might seem at first sight that the contradictory of 'William is wise' is 'William is not wise (or unwise)'. But this would assume that there is no other alternative, that William, and by implication everybody else, can be placed in one of two clearcut categories, the wise and the unwise. It seems fairly plain that we use the words 'wise' and 'unwise' much more loosely than this, that we do not on the whole classify everybody as one or the other and that any attempt to do so would neither make much sense nor fulfil any useful purpose.

At the same time we must not fall into the error of supposing that the difficulties of classification are due entirely to our lack of knowledge or of wisdom, that there is a right answer as to whether any given person is wise or unwise if only we could find it.

It is important to realise, in other words, that the reason why the classes are not clearcut is not merely, or even mainly, that we are not fully acquainted with the facts, but much more that the language, partly as a result of our trying to compress so much meaning into a single word, is inevitably shifting and vague. The nature of this vagueness is not easy to understand completely and we shall return to the point later. Perhaps the best way to think about it at this stage is that the words 'wise' and 'unwise' are useful but rather blunt and clumsy tools which sometimes help us to describe, vaguely, people and their actions, and which are often used to express approval or disapproval. There is nothing very much to be gained by trying to make them more precise.

There is a large number of pairs of words similar to 'wise' and 'unwise' in connection with which it may be interesting and perhaps important to consider whether they are in general used as contradictories or contraries or possibly neither. Very often the answer may be that it all depends on the context, sometimes they are, sometimes they aren't. Such pairs are rich, poor; strong, weak; right, wrong; rough, smooth; long, short; passive, active; legal, illegal. In general these are called *antonyms*, that is, words with opposite meanings, as contrasted with *synonyms*, which are words with the same meanings. But when words are called, loosely, antonyms it is not generally considered whether they are contradictories or contraries. Consider the pair 'rich, poor'. Although to some extent these may be used as relative terms, that is we might describe the same person as rich compared with one set of people and poor compared with another set, it would be unusual for the statements 'Smith is rich' and 'Smith is poor' both to be considered true at the same time about the same person. They could, however, perfectly well both be false; there are many people whom we would describe as neither rich nor poor. We would not in general say that everyone can be placed in one category or the other, though it would obviously be possible to lay down a definition whereby everyone whose income or wealth exceeded a certain figure was to be described as rich and everyone else as poor. In general, therefore, they are used as contraries, not contradictories, but it would not be difficult to lay down a use for them that would make them contradictories.

Consider 'right' and 'wrong'. In one set of uses, as applied to mathematical exercises, they are clearly contradictories. 56 is the *right* answer to the question: 'What is 7 times 8?' and every other answer is wrong. There is no answer that could be given that is neither right nor wrong. Perhaps because of our familiarity with this use there is a tendency to suppose that the words are also contradictories in other contexts. But there are a great many questions to which answers can be submitted which qualify for neither the 'right' nor the 'wrong' box. The question may be very complicated: 'What are the characteristics of an ideal society?' The answer may have to be qualified, 'It's a matter of opinion', 'It all depends'. And when we use the words 'right' and 'wrong' in a moral sense we do not generally use them as contradictories. There are a great many actions which we should describe as morally neutral.

An important point to consider with antonyms is whether the facts that are being described are such that there is a series of slight, continuous, possibly almost imperceptible changes, or whether there is a sudden change. If the changes are gradual it may also be important to consider whether they can be measured.

'On', 'Off' are antonyms which as applied for example to electric light switches are clearly contradictories. Click, and it's on; another click and it's off. There is nothing in between and the change is abrupt. Either it's on or it's off. 'Young', 'old' are antonyms describing facts where the changes are gradual and can be measured. As applied to people they are used relatively and loosely. A child might describe anyone over twenty as old; a centenarian might describe anyone under seventy as young. But on the whole they are used to describe ranges at the two ends of the scale, with a quite considerable range in between in which a person might be described as middle-aged. In other words they are normally used as contraries. If, however, for any purpose it is decided to call anyone of or above a certain age 'old' and anyone below it 'young' they would become contradictories. Two clear-cut classes, which are exclusive and exhaustive, can easily be defined.

'Hard', 'soft' are antonyms which, again, are used loosely. As applied to chairs or mattresses the changes described are gradual and cannot be measured easily, though no doubt a method of doing

65

so could be devised. On the whole they seem to be used as contraries.

In considering whether two antonyms are contradictories or contraries we note that if the classes they cover are exclusive and exhaustive the statements are contradictories; if the classes are exclusive and not exhaustive the statements are contraries. If the words are used in such a way as not to be exclusive then they are neither contradictories nor contraries, and it might be argued that they should not be described as antonyms.

In the exercise which follows the reader is asked to consider pairs of antonyms. In most cases it is not possible to be dogmatic about them, the answers are not clear-cut, they are often matters of opinion. The importance of considering them is that in doing so we have to think how we use the words and we are likely to come to a fuller understanding of the idea of contradictories and contraries.

Exercise 4.2

For the following pairs of words consider whether:

(a) they are generally used as contradictories, contraries, or neither;

(b) the changes described are gradual or sudden;

(c) if the changes are gradual, they can easily be measured.

If you think that it depends on the context you should say so, and explain.

1. intelligent, stupid.
2. passive, active.
3. present, absent.
4. solid, liquid.
5. fast, slow.
6. legal, illegal.
7. rough, smooth.
8. true, untrue.
9. wet, dry.
10. happy, unhappy.
11. certain, uncertain.
12. imprisoned, free.

'EITHER IT IS OR IT ISN'T'

An important point to emerge from the study of these antonyms is how often they are used as contraries, and how often the facts which are being described are subject to slight gradual changes, an indefinite number of imperceptible gradations over a range such as for example that which is covered by 'rough', 'smooth'.

A phrase which is often used, sometimes with the conviction on the part of the speaker that he is being ruthlessly logical, is 'Either it is or it isn't.' As applied to certain things, for example that motorcar being mine; that man being over 50; Robinson being present today; this may be perfectly reasonable or very nearly so. We might sometimes have to define carefully what we mean by Robinson being present, and it might be said that strictly speaking we can only make it necessarily true by our definitions, by putting the necessity in, by making it a closed system. But there are certainly a large number of examples where it will be a very misleading thing to say. 'Either Jones is or is not fit to play football' seems to imply that, as with the electric light switch, there is a click and he becomes at a certain stage in his convalescence fit to do certain things. We all know well that the facts are different, that the change is gradual, that the fitness is bound to be to some extent a matter of opinion. The 'either it is or it isn't' way of talking about it can be very unfortunate, for it can lead people to erroneous conclusions about the way things are, and cloud and confuse their thinking.

This is connected with the dangerous tendency for the study of formal thinking, of logic, to be confined to those cases where the divisions are clearcut, the rules rigid, in other words to be confined to a system that is closed, insulated from events in the real world. Such a practice produces answers that are right or wrong, and therefore in certain ways, for certain purposes—for example the setting of intellectual tests which can be easily corrected—may be thought to be more satisfactory. This clearcut 'logic' is then sometimes applied fallaciously, as with the 'Either it is or it isn't' examples, to things to which it is not properly applicable.

Two mistakes have here been made.

In the first place too much attention has been paid to closed system problems at the expense of the open system. Secondly—and this follows naturally—when our attention is turned to the open system we tend to tackle its problems with closed system methods which are certainly not always appropriate.

It cannot be repeated too often that the most important thinking that we have to do takes place in an open system, and that though we will to some extent use for this the methods and principles of a closed system, in many respects the assumptions, the techniques, the ways in which our minds operate will have to be different for clear and effective reasoning in actual, practical situations.

THE CONSTRUCTION OF CONTRADICTORIES
AND CONTRARIES

We examine now, briefly, what is involved in the construction of contradictories and contraries to a given statement.

Consider the statement 'Jane is over 40'. Jane's age is placed in a certain range 40–x, where there is theoretically no upper limit, and certainly no clearly defined one. The range 0–40 is excluded. The contradictory would be 'Jane is not over 40', which excludes the range that was before included and includes the one that was excluded. Between them these two statements exhaust the possibilities.

A contrary to the original statement would be 'Jane is under 30' or 'Jane is 27'. Notice that a contrary is necessarily more specific, gives more information than a contradictory. It selects a portion only of the range excluded by the original statement.

Consider now the statement 'Balbus built a wall'. There is no difficulty about the contradictory—'Balbus did not build a wall.' Whatever was asserted is denied. There may sometimes be a danger of ambiguities arising from certain positions of the negative. This may be avoided by saying 'It is not the case that . . .', or, in shorthand, 'Not (   )'. But in general the construction of the contradictory is automatic and it is not necessary to think about or to understand the meaning of the original.

A contrary, however, is more difficult. We have to deny that Balbus built a wall and we have to assert only a part of the range comprised in Balbus not building a wall. But as soon as we search for a contrary we see that we want to know what the context is, what the sentence is about, what particular information the speaker or writer is trying to get across. Is someone saying that it was *Balbus* who built the wall and not Marcus or Vergil or Horace? In which case, 'No, it was X' would be a contrary where X stands for anyone other than Balbus. Or is someone saying that it was a *wall* that Balbus built and not a crazy pavement or a rockery? Simply to say without knowing the context that 'Marcus built a wall' or 'Balbus built a crazy pavement' were contraries to 'Balbus built a wall' would clearly be unjustifiable, for it might be perfectly possible for each of them to be true at the same time as the original statement. It might often be necessary for the contrary to consist of more than one sentence if it is to be clear and unambiguous.

On the whole although it is important and helpful to one's thinking to understand the idea of contradictories and contraries, the construction of contraries is not a particularly useful operation. We note that it very often cannot be done without knowing the context of the original statement and this draws our attention to the danger of considering sentences in isolation. In studying the principles of thinking we want to examine sentences being *used* for communication or for reasoning, and they are always used in a context. 'Balbus built a wall' may be a useful sentence for grammarians or linguists to study in isolation, but a sentence in isolation is dead; the student of thinking wants to study sentences that are alive.

Exercises

4.3. Write down the contradictory and if possible a contrary of each of the following sentences. (Fill in whatever you think is necessary by way of background or context to make a contrary possible.)

1. At least some members of the Athenaeum are under 40.

2. $a \times b = y$.

3. Robinson lives at 27 Acacia Avenue.

4. No Hottentots play cricket.

5. Some of the red books in my library are by P. G. Wodehouse.

6. Arsenal won the F.A. Cup last year.

7. Only some members of the Larning Grammar School cricket eleven are also in the rugby fifteen.

8. Not all car drivers have licences.

4.4. Consider whether the following pairs of statements are equivalents (i.e. say the same thing), contradictories, contraries, or none of these things.

(Assume for the purposes of this question that fat, thin; tall, short; are pairs of contradictories):

1. (a) No thin people are tall.   (b) All tall people are thin.

2. (a) At least some short people are not fat.   (b) No short people are thin.

3. (a) All fat people are short.   (b) No tall people are fat.

4. (a) At least some thin people are not tall.   (b) Only some short people are fat.

4.5. The following statements are made, all about the same person:

1. He is a Mug.   3. He is a Blink.
2. He is a Wump.   4. He is a Blonk.

You are told that 1 and 2 are contradictories, that 2 and 3 are contraries, and that 1 and 4 are contraries. What can you say about 3 and 4?

Draw a diagram to show the relationships between Mugs, Wumps, Blinks and Blonks.

4.6. The following statements are all about the same object X:

1. X is A.   3. X is C.   5. X is E.
2. X is B.   4. X is D.

You are told that 3 and 5 are contradictories, that 2 and 4 are contraries, that 1 and 5 are contraries, and that 1 and 4 are contradictories.

You are also told that Y is not C.

What can you say about Y ?

Represent in a diagram the relationship between the classes A, B, C, D, E.

4.7. Boarding houses at a certain school are called by the initial letters of the alphabet—A, B, C, etc.; they are also called by the name of the building—The White House, The Brown House, etc.; and by the name of the housemaster.

Consider the following statements about which house a boy is in:
1. He is either in B House or the Green House.
2. He is either in A House, the White House or Mr Smith's House.
3. He is either in D House or Mr Jones's House.
4. He is either in the Yellow House or Mr Budd's House.
5. He is either in C House or the Red House.

(Assume that houses referred to in the same statement are all different. For example from 2 you know that A House, the White House and Mr Smith's House are three separate houses.)

You are told that: 1 and 2 are contradictories; 2 and 3 are contradictories; 3 and 4 are contraries; 4 and 5 are contraries.

You are also told that Mr Codd is not the housemaster of D House, and that Mr Budd is not the housemaster of the White House.

How many houses are there? Get as much information as you can about the names and the housemasters (they have not necessarily all been mentioned) of the various houses.

SUMMARY

1. Two statements are said to be contradictory if they cannot both be true and cannot both be false. They are said to be contrary if they cannot both be true but can both be false.

2. Words that are antonyms (e.g. 'wise' and 'unwise'), may be used as contradictories or as contraries or as neither. In considering which, it will often be important to think:

(a) whether the classes described are clearcut;

(b) whether the change from one to the other is sudden, or whether there is a large number of hardly perceptible gradations;

(c) whether the change can be measured numerically.

3. 'Either it is or it isn't' is a phrase that has to be watched carefully. It is often misleading.

4. In considering the contrary of a statement it may be very important to know the context and to be aware of the particular point that is being made.

Chapter 5

Labels

We have taken a look in the last chapter at some of the ways in which, and purposes for which, we put things into different categories. The things may be marbles put, literally, into different boxes according to their colour; they may be letters put into different files according to who wrote them; they may be activities put, metaphorically, into different compartments according to whether we approve of them; they may be people we know whose names will be put on different lists according to whether we are going to ask them to our party. In considering these classifications we have inevitably considered also the labels attached to the various boxes or categories, the words we use to describe them. We are now going to examine these words or labels in more detail. To some extent in doing so we shall be looking at our classifications again from a slightly different point of view, but we need make no apology for the element of repetition; the ideas we are considering form an essential base for all our thinking.

We make first two obvious points. The first is that words, language in general, are essential tools for almost all our thinking and communication above a very simple primitive level. It is an interesting psychological point to discuss and consider how much thinking does and can take place without words. There are certainly cases where it does and where it may indeed be exceedingly complicated, as for example over the chessboard. But most people seem to find that they can more effectively deal with their problems if they put them into words, perhaps on paper. And there is no doubt at all that whatever may be said about thinking without words, for communication with our fellow human beings words or their equivalent are almost indispensable. It is worth noting here in passing that although our thinking and communication may be made far more effective by a proper use of words, they may also be muddled and obscured as a result of a failure to understand just how language works and how it should be used. What constitutes a proper and what an improper use is something that we hope will emerge in the course of this book.

The second point is that language is constructed by mankind collectively for their convenience. They decided to which features of the world they found around them it would be convenient to attach labels, to give names. It was obviously vital for efficiency of communication that different people should call the same thing by the same name, and once an agreement to this effect had been built up it would be inconvenient to change it. But it would not be impossible. Over the years we find many examples of such changes, and we find also unfortunately many examples of misunderstandings, failures of communication, owing to the fact that the agreement to call the same things by the same names has not been effective. This point, that man should be the master of his language, may perhaps be seen more clearly if we remember to talk about what *we* mean by the words, or what we use them to mean, rather than what the words mean. It is sensible for us to try to use them consistently, but it is wise to note that this is not always done and that the meanings which words in fact convey are subject to variation and change.

OSTENSIVE DEFINITION

As we have already seen, classification, and therefore labelling, presents no difficulties when the distinctions are obvious and clear-cut. It must have been quite easy for man as he counted his fingers and thumbs to devise and agree upon names for the numbers one to ten. Most of the animals that man came across must have grouped themselves fairly obviously by their observed similarities and differences into categories to which labels could be attached. There would be no difficulty in instructing the young what the words 'tiger' and 'elephant' stood for. It would be done by showing or pointing. Such explanation of how a word is, or is to be, used is called *ostensive definition* (Latin *ostendo*=I show). Many objects today, for example modern motor-cars, have their labels literally attached to them. If we lacked experience of animal life we might be uncertain as to which of the cages marked respectively 'lion', 'tiger', 'leopard' was the correct one for a certain animal. But provided we could read we could have no doubt as to which if any of the enclosures marked 'Hillman', 'Austin', 'Triumph' was the right one for a car.

We have seen that there is almost no limit to the ways in which physical objects can be classified. They can be separated according to their nature (animate, four-legged, carnivorous), their size (over 1 ton), their origin (made in Japan), their purpose (to open bottles), their association with a person (belonging to Blenkinsop), their names (beginning with Q), or in innumerable other ways. The classification is normally undertaken because it is convenient for some particular purpose and sometimes, but by no means always, it is convenient to attach a label, a name, to the members of a particular category. As man's information about the animal world increased and became more specialised, so it was useful to have separate single words for the different categories or species. The label for tigers might have been 'rather like a cat, only bigger', but 'tiger' is shorter and more convenient. It has been suggested that once a single name is attached to the members of a particular category there is a danger of an over-elaborate investigation into some mysterious essence that they may be thought to hold in common. Suppose, for example, that for some purpose the class of Irishmen over six feet who disliked onions became important and significant, its members might be called 'grumphs' and this fact might give rise to speculation about the inner, essential nature of grumphness.

We give names to the categories of physical objects which we want to talk about often, and we can sometimes explain or define the names by pointing to the objects. To explain the class of those who dislike onions by pointing to a member of it will not be very helpful unless we can catch him in the act of spurning one. If we define a 'grumph' verbally we are merely drawing attention to classifications we have already made. We assume that the reader or listener knows that the whole class of men can be divided into Irishmen, Frenchmen, Englishmen, etc., that it can also be divided into those who are over 6 ft and those who are not; and that a classification of those who express themselves as disliking onions can also theoretically be made. To be a grumph is to belong to all these three classes. What is happening can be represented in a diagram thus:

The class of grumphs is represented by the shaded area.

It might very reasonably be objected here that though 'Irishmen' and 'those over 6 feet' are clearcut classes, or can easily be made so, 'disliking onions' is not. It is a matter of degree, it depends how they are cooked, and so on. The diagram is therefore misleading and it might have been better to have made the third qualification something clearcut like being under 40.

This brings us to the point that when we are combining several classifications of which the outlines are blurred the result is likely to be more blurred still. The class of small, sensible, affluent, middle-aged ladies would obviously be very far from clearcut and this would be one reason, but certainly not the only one, why nobody would be likely to want to attach a label to it.

It is important to realise that even in the cases where it would be quite easy to make our classifications and labelling clearcut there may be no particular advantage in doing so. Consider, for example, the class of physical objects made of wood, with a flat top, supported by three or four legs. Some of them will be called tables; some stools; some, perhaps, desks. The same object may have different labels at different stages of its career according to the purpose for which it is used. It is obviously right that this should be so, for purpose is one of the criteria of classification. But we do not want to be too fussy and precise in our ordinary everday living about the way in which we use the words. To insist on saying 'Pass me that stool' if I am going to sit on it, but 'Pass me that little table' if I am going to put my cup of tea on it would be pedantic and absurd.

We often have words for physical objects in which there is an overlap of this kind. There are some objects to which either word, 'table' or 'stool', might be applied, but there are many more which would only be called one or the other. Sometimes the label we choose to apply out of two or more alternatives may be determined by the structure of the object and sometimes by the purpose for which it is to be used. An investigation of the ways in which such words are used may reveal quite significant variations in the meanings which different people attach to them.

Exercises

5.1. Discuss the extent to which the following groups of words are used as:

(a) alternative labels for the same things (objects, activities, qualities, etc.), i.e. as synonyms;
(b) labels for nearly the same things;
(c) labels for the same things, but for different purposes;
(d) labels for different things.
(N.B. Start by thinking how *you* use them.)

1. cushion, pillow, bolster.
2. coat, jacket.
3. rock, stone.
4. jump, hop, leap.
5. juvenile, adolescent.
6. under, below.
7. chair, sofa.
8. road, lane.
9. bed, couch, divan.
10. bench, form.
11. staff, stick.
12. spade, shovel.

5.2. Consider to what extent it is possible to define the following words or phrases ostensively, that is without the use of any other words:

1. one hundred and eighty three.
2. mountain (distinguishing it from 'hill').
3. stream.
4. inside.
5. gross (adjective).
6. to ponder.
7. to reform.
8. Wednesday.
9. tomorrow.
10. ostensively.

VERBAL DEFINITION

The classification and labelling of physical objects, relationships, qualities, etc. do not raise many difficulties in principle, though there may be a large variety of problems concerning which classifications will be most convenient and suitable for particular purposes, and just where and how the dividing lines are to be drawn. There need be no basic confusion and muddle as long as we realise what we are doing and understand that there is no point in being more precise than our limited purposes require. When we come to the classification and labelling of ideas, and of things and aspects of things which cannot be ostensively defined, the situation is much more difficult.

I should have no difficulty in explaining to a foreigner how the word 'giraffe' is used, provided that there is a specimen available, or even the picture of one, to which I can point. This would be so even though we do not understand a single word of each other's language. But I would find it very difficult indeed to explain to him how the word 'honourable' is used. Even if I could parade before him examples of people doing honourable things how could I direct his attention to those particular aspects of their behaviour which are covered by the word? In suggesting it we see how absurd the attempt would be and we are further driven to reflect upon just what aspects of behaviour we do call honourable. How, if at all, do we distinguish them from those which we call honest?

If I am explaining the use of the word to someone who speaks English but has never come across 'honourable' before I would have to do it mostly in words, and perhaps by calling his attention to examples, with which I know him to be familiar, of behaviour which I would call honourable. To explain how one word is used in terms of other words is called *verbal definition*, and it is of course what is done in all dictionaries.

Verbal definition is obviously circular. We look up 'brave' and find it means 'courageous': we look up 'courageous' and find it means 'brave'. It will only be effective in bringing understanding to the hearer or reader when most, if not all, of the other words used are familiar to him and are known to refer to something that is within his experience. We can never succeed in explaining what pink looks like in words (or in any other way) to someone who has been blind from birth.

Words such as 'honour', 'courage', 'goodness', for which there is no corresponding concrete physical object, are often called 'abstract' words. As we have already suggested, their use and their understanding are considerably more difficult than those of words which are labels for material objects. It may be helpful if we consider how we come to learn how they are used.

Once a child has acquired a skeleton vocabulary of those words which refer to everyday objects and activities, and has learnt to read, he will be adding to his collection of words the whole time by listening and reading. There will be many occasions when the isolated word is unfamiliar but its meaning can be guessed at from the context. The word crops up again and its new context provides confirmation or otherwise of what we understood by it the first time. Sometimes we look it up in the dictionary, but dictionaries are not used enough when we are learning our own language. We collect a large number of uses of the same word in different contexts and by a process, which is only partly conscious, of comparing and seeing what the uses seem to have in common, we come to a conclusion about the range of ideas which this word can be used to cover. The conclusions to which different people come will by no means always be the same, and most people have probably had the experience of looking up a word in the dictionary, perhaps almost by accident, and discovering that what they have been understanding by it is significantly different from what the dictionary says. It would be sensible then to try to discover whether the way in which other people use it agrees with them or with the dictionary.

The more we think about it the more clearly we see that there is an inevitable, but not necessarily regrettable, lack of precision about the ways in which abstract words are used.

We are not always precise, often because we do not want to be, when we talk about material objects. This lack of precision, and some of the ways in which it is made worse when we are dealing with abstract ideas, may be illustrated by an example.

Imagine a very large number of pebbles of different shapes, sizes, weights, colours. Each one is unique. We could classify them in many different ways according to their properties and attach labels and names to the various categories. The complete and detailed classification would have to have as many categories as there are pebbles; there would have to be a different label for each one if we are to describe them accurately. This would not be very difficult to do by giving numerical values to the various grades within the categories of, for example, weight, length, girth, etc. A label might then read something like this: 'A12/4. E373/2. X19'. In such a case our labelling is precise and there would be no difficulty in ensuring agreement between those who write and those who read the labels that they mean and understand the same things by them. In fact these labels perform efficiently their job of communicating.

Suppose, however, that we were unable or were not allowed to measure the properties of the pebbles such as their weight, length, etc. but were only allowed to use a limited number of categories such as large, heavy, long. It is easy to see that our descriptions then would be imprecise. Without measurement it would be very difficult to have an effective agreement as to how these labels were to be used. The exact range covered by each category would be impossible to define, and the labels might be describing, necessarily vaguely, several things at once—for example weight as well as length.

This example illustrates some of the difficulties we have when we attach a label such as 'brave' to some person or action. Clearly the entities (people and their actions) to which the adjective might be applied are indefinitely numerous and each one of them is unique. There is no way of measuring what we are describing, and ensuring that there shall be agreement about meaning. Suppose for example that I call your attention to someone's course of action and ask 'Was that brave or courageous?' Neglecting for the moment the possibility of your saying 'neither', how would you decide between the two? These words are nearly synonymous. I would use them more or less indiscriminately, having a slight preference for the adjective 'brave' and the noun 'courage', but this preference is one of euphony and has nothing to do with the meaning I would attach to them if using them or understand by them if hearing or reading them. It is perfectly possible, however, that some people may make a distinction between them, though it is likely to be a subtle one. In this case their communication with me or mine with them will be slightly defective. But the essential point for our present purposes is that there is no right answer though there may be one (I suggest 'it doesn't matter') which is fairly generally agreed. It is interesting that for the clearcut classes of physical objects, such as thrushes and blackbirds, we do not on the whole have synonyms; one label is sufficient. But the English language abounds in synonyms or near-synonyms for more abstract ideas. Ideally these words would be used to express subtly different aspects of the same notion and to some extent they are. But as we have already suggested it is very difficult indeed for an agreement to be built up whereby different people will understand the same subtly different aspect by the same word, and very difficult also to discover to what extent it has been built up.

There is the further point that when we call somebody or some action 'brave' we may well be describing several things at once with some uncertainty as to what they are. Are we thinking only of what was actually done, or are we aiming to say something about the motive, or to what extent the individual had to exercise his will-power to perform it? Is it *always* brave to ski straight down a slope of 1 in 3 or does it depend on who does it and when?

Words that are used like this, as abstract words often are, to convey information about several different categories at once are often called 'blanket' or 'portmanteau' words. (The metaphor is obvious: they cover or contain several different meanings or kinds of information.) Such words may be useful when precision is not important or not possible, they may provide a helpful shorthand. But they can also be dangerously misleading.

It is in general inevitable that the area of description of abstract words should be uncertain, shifting, loose, and often it may not matter that this is so. The essential thing is to be aware of it, to understand its inevitability and to see the nature of the lack of precision and the reasons for the blurred outline. And we note the obvious fact that we can often clarify the outline, put it in sharper focus by giving more details if they are available. To specify more categories, even though measurement is not possible and outlines are blurred, may well give a clearer picture.

Another reason why the word picture may be confusing is that words are often used not merely to describe the facts but to express the attitude of the speaker. If I ask whether the food you had for breakfast was bacon or sausages I am enquiring about the facts; if I go on to ask whether it was nice or nasty I am enquiring about your attitude to it, whether you liked it or not. When we are talking our attitude to what is being described may often be conveyed partly by tone of voice or by expression. In writing it can be done only by the choice of words. In dealing with abstract words, whether in speech or on paper, it may be very difficult to disentangle the facts from the attitude. There is no difficulty about your breakfast; you had sausages and you didn't like them. But if I describe someone as 'reasonable' it is very hard to say to what extent I am describing the facts and to what extent giving information about my attitude to them. The words or expressions which are clearly factual, whether precise or not (over 75 years old; a middle-aged brunette), or those which clearly express an attitude (enjoyable; my favourite view), present no difficulties in this respect. But those which do both, when it is not clear to what extent they are doing which, may be seriously misleading. A good illustration of what is happening is provided by the well-known conjugation: 'I am determined; you are obstinate; he is pig-headed.' A resolution not to be deflected from one's purpose is described in oneself with unqualified approval; in the person with whom one is talking, and perhaps disagreeing, it is described with moderate disapproval; and in a third person, who is absent and may therefore be insulted with impunity it is described with an almost angry contempt.

Again, if we are considering whether Smith's action was brave or foolhardy then provided we are in possession of the full facts of the case, we can only be investigating our attitude to those facts.

EMOTIVE USE OF WORDS

Words are obviously often used with the intention of making a difference to other people's attitudes. There are certain words which by constant association with pleasant or unpleasant things automatically arouse emotions of approval or disapproval in most people. In such cases the processes of thinking may be eliminated or nearly so. This is called the *emotive* use of words.

Such words as 'wanton' or 'crass' do not, as generally used today, add much information about what is being described; in fact many people might have some difficulty in giving their dictionary definitions. They are terms of abuse, indicating that the speaker or writer is angrily disapproving and intends to arouse similar emotions in the listener or reader. There are many words to which certain people will automatically and unthinkingly react in a hostile manner, perhaps especially political words. Examples are: progressive, reactionary, doctrinaire, capitalist (bloated), communist.

Sometimes a word which originally described with some accuracy an activity of which almost everyone disapproves (for example, 'murder', 'rape', 'blackmail') is used metaphorically (or just inaccurately) about something different with the intention of transferring the disapproval. ('Everybody automatically views murder with disgust; we want them to view this with disgust; so let's call it murder.') People therefore talk about the English language being murdered when it is used in a way that they don't like. They talk about the countryside being raped if a building is erected which spoils their view. They talk about an act of blackmail if someone makes a threat of which they disapprove.

People may also try hard to arouse automatic emotions of approval by the use of a word or phrase. Advertisers are doing this when they search for an effective brand name. When they call a certain bread 'Mother's Pride' the hope is that automatically, unthinkingly, perhaps unconsciously, the public will feel favourably disposed towards it. There has recently been some discussion about the desirability of resale price maintenance. Obviously if a policy (like a commercial product) has attached to it a name which automatically arouses emotions of approval it is more likely to be supported by the public. A national newspaper which is in favour of resale price maintenance has been calling it to start with 'resale price maintenance (Fair Trade)', and then later 'Fair Trade (resale price maintenance)'. The descriptive title is gradually being replaced by the one which also expresses an opinion.

Obviously the essential thing as far as our thinking is concerned is to be aware of what is happening; not to mistake an enquiry about attitudes or opinions for one about facts; and to be on our guard against the sometimes irrational effect on our attitudes that the use of words in this way may have. The child who continually hears a pudding being described as nasty is not likely to feel favourably disposed towards it, but the fact that some others dislike it—or perhaps one person who says so often—is no reason why he should. He is less likely to be affected if he is conscious that the word 'nasty' only gives information about an attitude, and not about the pudding. Similarly we must try to sort out the subtler cases, and distinguish what we are being told about the object, the idea, the quality, the person, from what we are being told about the speaker's or writer's attitude to it. It may be helpful if we think of the verbal picture not merely (as with a camera) as a picture of what is described, but one in which the man describing it, and liking or disliking, approving or disapproving, is included.

WORDS WITH DIFFERENT MEANINGS

A common cause of misunderstanding, muddled thinking or fallacious argument is the use of the same word with slightly different meanings. To take a simple and trivial example: if I am told that two people are both reading the same book I would not know whether they were reading identically the same copy—perhaps taking it in turns or looking over each other's shoulder, or whether they were reading two separate copies of the same work. In this case the misunderstanding would be unlikely to matter much, but the fact that 'same' is used to mean either identically the same ('We both went to the same football match'), or very closely similar, perhaps exactly alike ('I see that Brown and Green are both wearing the same tie'), has often been a source of muddle. Meanings

83

which are widely different are not very likely to give rise to ' misunderstandings, they are much more likely to be the source of jokes. When the electricity bill is called the Charge of the Light Brigade, the jest, such as it is, depends on ambiguities in the words 'charge' and 'light'. A very large number of words in the English language are used with two or more different meanings, and a large proportion of jokes are based on these ambiguities. The important point so far as our thinking is concerned is that when we are examining a piece of reasoning we should be aware of the possibility of mistakes or fallacies resulting from the same word or phrase being used to mean different things, perhaps only very slightly different, in the same argument.

Exercises

5.3. Discuss the extent to which the following groups of words are used as synonyms or near-synonyms:
1. modest, humble, simple.
2. dreadful, fearful, frightful.
3. disgusting, revolting.
4. rebuke, correct.
5. understand, comprehend.

5.4. Consider whether the following words are likely to be used to describe attitudes or opinions as well as facts:
1. liberty, licence.
2. complacent, satisfied.
3. precocious.
4. callow.

5.5. Which of the following adjectives describe properties that can be measured with reasonable accuracy?
1. loud.
2. intelligent.
3. sane.
4. full.
5. comfortable.
6. beautiful.

5.6. Discuss why it is that people feel a name to be more personal and individual than a number although there may be many John Smiths and only one BM/XYZ. 193745.

5.7
1. A 'quoojum' is defined as a man of thirty or over, who has been to the North Pole, has travelled at over 800 m.p.h. in a plane and lives in Rutland.

If a man goes to the North Pole, travels at over 800 m.p.h. by plane, and settles in Rutland, does he become a quoojum on his thirtieth birthday?

2. 'Fleas' are defined in the *Concise Oxford Dictionary* as 'small wingless jumping insects feeding on human and other blood'. If you take a small insect, cut off its wings, teach it to jump and train it to feed on human and other blood does it become a flea?

5.8. In each of the following groups of near-synonyms which would you regard as (a) implying approval, (b) implying disapproval, (c) neutral:

1. enormous, inordinate, unconscionable, stupendous, terrific.
2. conceal, keep secret, suppress, screen.
3. security services, secret police.
4. restrain, check, curb, shackle.
5. withdraw, retreat, retire, go back.
6. moderate, mediocre, average, golden mean.

5.9. Consider the soundness of the following arguments:

1. A man who is not free is a slave. I have just been told that I am not free to build my own house wherever I would like to. Therefore I am a slave.

2. You say you want an editor whose politics are independent. I have formed my political views entirely independently and will continue to do so. In this respect at least therefore I can claim to be a suitable candidate for the post.

SUMMARY

In considering the labelling of the categories into which we put objects, ideas, qualities, etc., or the words which we use to describe them, the following main points have emerged:

1. Words are essential tools for thinking and for communication.

2. But we must remember that language is constructed by man for man's convenience, and we must see to it that we retain the mastery, that we adjust our language to our thinking and not the other way round.

3. The explanation of the labelling of physical objects is done on the whole by *ostensive definition*: sometimes we want these labels to

give precise information, very often it does not matter if the information is only vague.

4. When, as with abstract ideas, we are unable to point or show we have to use *verbal definition*. This is bound to be circular and much less precision is possible. Again this may not matter, but it is important to be aware of it.

5. The main reasons for this inevitable lack of precision and the resulting fuzziness of communication are:

(a) What is being described often cannot be measured. It is important to realise that this is not merely because we don't know how to measure, but because there are some things which of their nature do not admit of measurement.

(b) It is very difficult to ensure that different people will use the same word in the same way, and very difficult also to know whether or not they are doing so.

(c) We often use a single 'blanket' or 'portmanteau' word to cover a description of many different kinds.

(d) Words are often used to describe not only the facts but also the attitudes and opinions of the speakers or writers.

6. Mistakes in reasoning may result from the same word being used in different senses at different stages of an argument. Slight differences of meaning here are much more dangerous than wide ones. In an argument which we feel sure is wrong, but can't quite see why, we will often find this type of fallacy.

7. The clearest and most helpful way to look at it is to think not so much of the meanings which the words have but of the tasks of communication for which they are used. And we must often separate here the job which they are meant to do, the meaning that is intended, from the job which they in fact do, the meaning that is communicated.

Chapter 6

Statements

We say and write things of many different kinds for many different purposes. Although in detail these purposes vary greatly it would seem safe to say that they can be covered generally by the loose, broad categories of *thinking* (using the word in the sense in which it includes reflecting and remembering) and *communicating*. In everything that we say or write we are talking to ourselves or talking to other people, or possibly both, for the categories are not exclusive, though they are, at least nearly, exhaustive.

It is obvious that our utterances and writings can be further analysed and classified in an almost indefinite number of different ways. As we have already pointed out, classification is not of itself a particularly useful operation; we only want to do it if we can see that it serves or might serve some purpose in which we are interested. We shall suggest in this chapter certain distinctions which will help us to think more clearly, distinctions such that if we fail to understand them we are likely to get into a muddle.

Before doing this it will be useful to make a general point which arises from the broad classification of the purposes of speech and writing into thinking and communicating.

Everything that is said or written is the product of a particular person or group of people on a particular occasion, and generally for a particular purpose. This is obviously true when we are dealing with the spoken word, and it may sometimes be very misleading indeed to consider a sentence in isolation from actual and possible contexts. The sentence, for example, 'This orange is yellow' might be used by grammarians or logicians to demonstrate a grammatical point or as a type of sentence attributing a certain property to an object. This may be a perfectly sensible and useful thing to do, but if we start analysing in detail just what the sentence says we must remember that the answer is—'it all depends'. It depends on who said it, when, and for what purpose. And the purpose, the object of saying it, will very often be made clear by the stresses, the tone of voice, of the speaker. It is possible of course that someone may be wandering round the room attributing properties to objects, picking up various things and making remarks such as: 'This book is red', 'This clock ticks', 'This banana is unripe', 'This bottle is empty', but it is more likely that a sentence such as 'This orange is yellow' would be uttered to make a specific point. It might be a complaint, implying that it is therefore unripe ... how can you expect me to eat it? It might be pointing a contrast with all the other oranges in the bowl. It might be to give an example of what the colour yellow looks like, or what the word 'yellow' is used to mean, to someone who doesn't understand the language. It might be said emphatically: 'It *is* yellow', to someone who denies it and appears to be colour blind. It would on the whole only be linguists or philosophers, using it as an exhibit, a specimen, who would imagine it being used tonelessly. But the tone or the stress may be the most important thing about it. To disregard the context, the speaker, the audience, the purpose, the *particular* point that is being made, could be at least misleading.

Exercise 6.1

Suggest different contexts in which the following sentences might be spoken and indicate how they might be stressed differently according to the purposes for which they are being used.

(Think about the possible preceding questions or remarks. Ask yourself exactly what information the speaker might be trying to get across.)

1. This table is flat.
2. This knife is sharp.
3. The pram seems to be empty.
4. Cows moo.
5. The door is shut.
6. I've found a caterpillar.

When we are writing we are unable to convey information by our tone of voice or by stressing particular words or sentences. It is true that we may occasionally underline words, but this is less effective and less subtle than what can be done by inflections or even by gestures, and is a device that is not greatly used. On the whole we have to convey the different stresses by elaborating, perhaps lengthening, the sentence or altering its shape.

Consider for example the sentence 'Jane is married to John'.

This might be the answer to any of the questions 'Who's married to John?', 'To whom is Jane married?', 'Are Jane and John related?', and in speaking we would stress either 'Jane' or 'John' or 'married' according to which question we were answering. In writing we could achieve the emphasis on Jane or John by saying 'It's Jane who's married to John', or 'It's John to whom Jane is married', but it is less easy to shape the sentence to emphasise 'married'. We might do it by saying, 'John and Jane are husband and wife', but opinions would perhaps differ as to whether this effectively shifts the emphasis where it is wanted.

When a sentence is written, perhaps especially when it is printed in a book, it seems more natural to think of it as a general statement addressed to the world at large rather than as a product of a particular person with particular purposes. But although the context will be larger and the purposes more general it will still be the case that the writer will be trying to perform particular acts of communication—to instruct, to persuade, to explain, to inform or whatever else it may be. And a particular sentence or group of sentences must normally be considered in its context following from and leading up to the surrounding sentences and paragraphs, as a part of the whole article or chapter or book. To forget, when we are analysing or examining a statement, that when it is used the most important thing about it is that it is part of a larger whole, would be like a biologist examining a severed limb and forgetting that the most important thing about it is that it was once part of a living body. But just as the biologist can learn much about bodies and about life by dissecting and examining separate limbs, so we can learn much about thinking by analysing the separate statements of which a train of thought is made up. If we never considered anything by itself without at the same time considering the whole of which it is a part, if we looked only at the whole landscape and never at the separate bits of which it is composed, our view would be hopelessly general and blurred and we would neither know where to go nor how to get there. But we must be on the alert to remember about the whole body, the context, the surrounding landscape, we must think to what extent they make a difference to what we are considering, and we must, where it is necessary and appropriate, make allowances.

In this chapter we are undertaking an examination of statements and a classification of them as far as seems to be useful for our present purposes. Inevitably we must consider them to some extent in isolation, but we must be aware of the fact that they draw their life blood from their contexts, the particular situation in which they are used.

We have talked rather loosely about the contexts and purposes of sentences or statements. The classification 'sentences' normally includes questions, requests, expressions of surprise and pleasure as well as statements of the type 'A is B'. The classification 'statements' normally includes only those sentences in which something is asserted, something is said to be so. A distinguishing feature is that a statement is a sentence of which it at least makes sense to ask whether it is true or false, whereas it makes no sort of sense to ask whether a question or a request is true or false. It is with statements that we are now to be concerned.

The first classification that it is convenient to make is of those statements which say something about the world of experience, the world in which we live. They might be described as open system statements. For example: 'Buggins robbed a bank yesterday'; 'It's snowing'; 'Jones is taller than Smith'; 'The sun will shine this afternoon'. These statements may be about the past, the present or the future. They may be true or false, and on the whole we would set about discovering which by investigation. Most statements are of this kind.

Our second category is of statements which say something about an artificial world of our own construction, or statements which are definitions. These are closed system statements. 'A bishop (at chess) moves diagonally'; 'There are twelve inches in a foot', are examples. When the game of chess was invented it was agreed or decreed that that was how a bishop should move. It was made true. And there is no question or possibility of discovering any exceptions to it. Similarly, 'There are twelve inches in a foot', was made true by definition. It might have been decided that there should be ten inches in a foot, indeed this may still be decided in the future, in which case the size either of an inch or of a foot or possibly both, will have to be altered. It might be said that the statement is really a declaration to the effect that there is a general agreement in our community to call this length a foot, and to call one-twelfth of this length an inch.

These two types of statement are sometimes called *empirical* (which means 'derived from experience'), and *analytic* respectively. It may be helpful to think of them as Discovery statements and Agreement statements.

It may be a matter of considerable importance to decide whether a given statement is empirical or analytic, or to what extent it is one or the other. The same form of words may be empirical in one set of circumstances and analytic in another. The question to ask will be whether, and if so how, the truth of the statement can be tested. We have seen that analytic statements are, if true, necessarily true. They are true by agreement. It is of course the case that we may want to test whether the agreement is as stated. But the method of testing the truth of 'A bishop (at chess) moves diagonally' will be of a rather different kind from that of testing the truth of 'The bishop of Barchester moves with a limp'. In the first case we look up the rules of chess, in the second we make enquiries about or go and look at the bishop of Barchester.

Another example may help to elucidate the point. Suppose that Smith says or writes: 'Every civilised person to whom I have spoken regards the Government's proposals with horror.' At first sight this might appear to be an empirical statement which we could check by interviewing the civilised people to whom Smith has spoken. But it would obviously be reasonable to enquire what the qualifications are for being civilised. If we find that one of the qualifications, in Smith's eyes, is to regard the Government's proposals with horror, then clearly the statement has a 'built-in irrefutability'; it is bound to be true. Smith himself clearly regards the expression of horror in this matter as a mark of a civilised man, and it would therefore be quite natural for him to treat it as part of the definition. It might be said that in his conversations with people he is testing them for being civilised, he is not testing whether his statement is true. In other words if Smith is not going to allow his statement to be false, if any apparent exception that is produced is discarded as not being what *he* calls a civilised person, the statement becomes analytic, a matter of definition, necessarily true, not testable by experience. What is happening when a statement is made necessarily true is summed up neatly in the old Elizabethan epigram:

'Treason doth never prosper. What's the reason?
For if it prosper none dare call it treason.'

A great many statements of this kind are made and though it might be unfair to claim that their authors are making them completely analytic, not allowing them to be false in any circumstances, it is often the case that they are more nearly a matter of definition than would appear on the surface. In such cases they do not really give information about the world of experience apart from the speaker; they merely tell us about his attitude. In the example we have been considering we would certainly be left in no doubt as to the fact that Smith regards the proposals with horror and expects other people to do so too. Perhaps it would be better if he simply said this, but by expressing it in a form where it appears to be empirical, about other people, he gives the statement, at least superficially, a greater authority. Other people may feel that they too ought to express horror in order to qualify as civilised.

We see then that the information given by a statement may be of several different kinds. It may be about an agreement or a definition; it may be about the speaker; or it may be about the world outside the speaker. Information under these different headings will often be combined in the same statement, and it may then be a matter of some importance to disentangle the various elements.

Exercise 6.2
Consider and if necessary discuss whether the following statements are likely to be empirical (discovery; testable by investigation), or analytic (agreement or definition; not allowed to be false). Think in each case of the kind of information that it is likely to be intended to give, and that it is likely in fact to give:

1. A quadruped has four legs.
2. A fly has six legs.
3. There is no mountain in the British Isles over 5,000 feet high.
4. There is no mountain in the British Isles less than 500 feet high.
5. The weight of Robinson is 200 lb.
6. The weight of 1 lb is 16 ounces.
7. 'In countries where they know how to deal with winter cold, windows in homes and offices are always double glazed.' (Advertisement)
8. 'The names of the advertisers are those of the most reputable firms in the country.' (Claim by *Daily Express*)

9. 'No wonder so many distinguished people write their letters on Basildon Bond.' (Advertisement)

10. 'What I, for my part, never meet is an educated and/or naturally intelligent person who feels that his own point of view is represented by either the Conservative or the Labour Party, let alone those inefficiently professional representatives of the unrepresented, the Liberals.' (Letter to *The Times*)

11. 'Over-centralisation is the enemy of efficiency.'

NECESSITY AND CERTAINTY

A natural corollary of the difference between statements about the world of experience whose truth we discover, and statements whose truth we make, is that there will obviously be an important difference between the degrees or rather between the kinds of certainty which we can attach to them. When we agree that there shall be three feet in one yard that statement is necessarily true as long as the agreement holds. When we *make* it true it is in fact better to talk about necessity than about certainty. Being certain or uncertain is a psychological state admitting of degrees. I am more certain that the sun will rise tomorrow morning than that the postman will call. Most people in fact would describe themselves as completely certain about the first of these, though they might admit, under pressure, that it is *possible* that the world might come to an end during the night. How certain we feel about whether various things have happened, are happening or will happen, depends on the evidence and also on our individual natures. Some people are sceptical and may feel doubtful on the same evidence that persuades others to feel certain. In other words statements about the world of experience will be regarded with various degrees of doubt and certainty; but analytic statements, which are expressions of agreement are, if true, necessarily so.

STATEMENTS OF FACT AND OF OPINION

We come now to a further classification of statements which are or appear to be about the world of experience.

Consider the two statements:

1. Jones is wearing glasses. 2. Jones has an attractive personality.

The first would be generally agreed to be a statement of fact which may be true or false.

93

The second would normally be described as a matter of opinion. If someone disagreed with it the natural reaction would be, not to say that either he or the original speaker was wrong, but that each of them was perfectly entitled to his opinion. Notice that it might be rephrased either: '*I* find Jones's personality attractive', or 'Most people find . . .', or possibly 'I and most other people find . . .'. In these cases the statements are of fact whose truth or falsehood may be discovered by investigation.

It is obvious that this distinction between statements of fact and of opinion is important. It may matter very much whether we are being told something about the world of experience outside the speaker or whether we are merely being given information about a particular, limited set of facts, the state of mind of the speaker. But it may not always be very easy to make the distinction. It will help us to come to a conclusion as to the category into which to put a given statement if we consider whether the speaker is describing a mental or emotional relationship between himself and some other person or object; we want to think whether we would try to verify the statement by investigating the object that is being described or the speaker's and other minds.

If someone says: 'This cake weighs over 2 lb', there is no doubt that it is the cake which we want to investigate. But if someone says: 'This cake is nice', although it is true that we might feel that we wanted to taste the cake in order to see what our opinion is, we would not think that our not liking it would be sufficient to disprove the statement. We should want to ask the speaker whether he merely means that *he* likes it, or whether he is also saying that other people do in fact, or probably would, like it too. In saying this he might be expressing an opinion, making a judgment, about other people's tastes.

This brings us to a further important distinction. When we ask someone for his opinion we may want to know what his taste is, whether he likes it, as when we ask someone to taste the cake; or we may be asking someone what his judgment is as when we ask for his opinion as to how heavy the cake is. In the first case we are asking what the facts are about his taste-reactions, pleasurable or otherwise, to the cake; the facts are private facts and there is certainly no simple way, perhaps no way, of testing his answer against them. In the second case we are asking for his judgment about a

94

matter of fact which is public; whether it is a good judgment, that is an accurate or nearly accurate one, can easily be discovered by weighing the cake.

VALUE JUDGMENTS

A statement which assesses the merits or comparative merits of people, things or ideas is usually called a value judgment.

This phrase is inevitably used loosely and its employment may often to some extent conceal a difficult, important and controversial issue. We have just considered cases where the distinction was clear between a statement of fact ('This cake is heavier than that') and a statement of opinion or taste ('I prefer this cake to that'). Let us take an example where the distinction is rather less clear.

Suppose a schoolmaster says: 'This essay is better than that.' Is his statement one of fact or of opinion? Is he assessing something which is public like the weight of a cake or something which is private like the effect of a cake on his sense of taste. To analyse this in detail is a complicated matter; most people, however, would probably agree that what he is doing is to some extent a mixture of the two kinds of judgments.

It is important to understand the distinctions between fact and opinion, and between taste and judgment, but it would be a great mistake to suppose that it is possible to say that all statements can be placed in one or other of clearcut categories of this kind. To try to do so would be likely to lead to a distortion of the meanings that statements were intended to carry and would be a great waste of time and intellectual energy. A better way of thinking of it is to see that in the statements we make there are these various elements— agreements or definitions, information about the world of experience, expressions of taste, judgments about present or past facts, predictions about what people's tastes will be and about future events in general. And these predictions may shade over into recommendations as to what should be done in order to achieve certain purposes. It will help us to think more effectively if we understand these elements, and by distinguishing between them see more clearly what it is that is being done. The two questions that we want to keep on asking ourselves are 'What exactly is it that he is trying to *say*?' and 'What would one have to do, what sort of evidence would one want, in order to verify the statement?'

Examples

It may be useful now if we undertake an examination and analysis of some passages on the lines we have suggested.

1. *'Over half of Britain's exports depend on steel.'* At first sight this might appear to be a simple statement of fact which must be true or false. But when we come to consider how we would verify it, we want to know rather more about how the phrase 'depend on' is being used. Does it mean that they are made, at least partly, of steel? Or does it mean that steel is used in the process of manufacturing them, that the machinery or factory which turns them out is partly made of steel? Or that the vehicles which are used to transport them are made of steel? We can see that it would be quite easy to use 'depend on' in such a wide way as to ensure that the statement is true, and to make it impossible for anyone to challenge it. But the statement then, obviously, says very little.

2. 'The —— are putting into the field for the next election a team of candidates who are more numerous, more intelligently progressive and generally more attractive than ever before. If the electorate shows the usual innate good sense of the British public the result will be a marked increase in the number of —— M.P.s.'

The first sentence starts with a statement of fact ('more numerous ... than ever before') which could easily be tested. 'More intelligently progressive' is clearly a matter of opinion (*taste* rather than *judgment*); what strikes me as 'progressive' may strike you as 'doctrinaire'. This could hardly be tested; even if a majority of people agreed it would not mean very much unless the terms were more clearly defined. We note, however, that it is certainly intended as a term of commendation. 'Generally more attractive' is ambiguous, but it would seem reasonable to suppose that 'attractive to the electorate' is what is meant. In this case it is a prediction whose accuracy will be tested at the election.

The second sentence is put in such a form as to be irrefutable. It is therefore analytic. If there proves not to be a marked (whatever that may mean) increase in the number of M.P.s the electorate clearly cannot have shown their good sense; the *test* of 'showing good sense' is made to be the return of a certain number of —— candidates.

When we ask the reader in the exercises below to sort out the different elements in sentences and collections of sentences, it does not follow that there is the implication that the passage is open to criticism. The object is to give practice in the very important skill of recognising what is analytic, what is empirical, and distinguishing between fact, taste and judgment. When the various strands have been recognised the reader may or may not feel that there is ground for adverse criticism.

Exercise 6.3

Consider and discuss the extent to which the various elements of fact, taste, judgment, etc., are to be found in the following statements. (Think, in each case, how you would test them.)

1. This chair is comfortable.
2. 'Nothing pleases so much as Players.'
3. 'Only the coffee bean gives such delicious fragrance and flavour with such deep warm comfort.'
4. Chess is the best of all indoor games.
5. Robinson is the acknowledged expert in this matter.
6. 'Fascinating reading, a beautifully produced book with over 200 colour photographs and maps.'
7. 'Travel writing is most readable when it records disasters.'
8. Too much hard work never did anybody any harm.
9. 'The delirious London majority in the crowd were entitled to their wild celebration, for their men were in the finish the worthy winners.' (*The Observer*)
10. 'His chipping showed admirable touch, control and understanding of the bigger ball's characteristics.' (*The Observer*)
11. '—— are famous throughout the world as the pioneers of the automatic washing machine. —— technical superiority guarantees that theirs is the finest washing and drying action incorporated in any washing machine. The —— name is known by *every* housewife in the country.' (Advertisement)
12. 'There is an increasing, and most welcome, general demand for full-time post-secondary education. There exist at present to cope with the demand the technical colleges and colleges of further education, which vary widely in what they do, but tend to be vocationally specialised in their courses and to lack glamour; the teacher training colleges, which do what their name implies; and the universities. Collectively they are not adequate for the purpose. But

because the demand is on the whole commendable and because it on the whole contributes to the formation of the sort of technically competent society which everyone has in view, the demand deserves to be met.' (*The Times*)

SUMMARY
1. The word 'statement' is usually applied to those sentences which assert something that can be true or false.
2. Such statements can be analytic, that is agreement or definition statements, which, if true, are necessarily so (closed system statements).
3. Or they can be empirical, about the world of experience (open system statements).
(Some statements which appear to be empirical may be given a built-in irrefutability, or nearly so, by the fact that the writer or speaker is defining his terms in such a way as not to allow his statement to be false. It is important to be able to see when this is happening.)
4. Or they can merely give information about the speaker's attitude or tastes. (It would be a matter of definition, and of no great significance, whether these should be called empirical.)
5. One of the most important points to consider when we are investigating a statement is whether its truth can be tested, and if so how.
6. Some statements assert facts, and some give opinions.
7. Opinions may be matters of taste or of judgment, or some combination of the two.
8. What are ordinarily called value judgments may be about things which are agreed to be matters of taste, or they may be judgments of merit which some people would hold to be matters of fact.
9. It is suggested that the most helpful way to think about these distinctions is not as clearcut categories but as elements which are likely to be found in the statements that are made. The ability to recognise and understand these elements should assist us to think more clearly.

Chapter 7

The Structure of Reasoning–1

When we say things like 'If . . . then . . .', 'because . . . therefore . . .', we are making the claim that from one proposition or state of affairs something else follows. The nature of this link, the reason why it follows, can vary considerably. We are now going to examine in some detail the structure of reasoning of the type represented by 'If . . . then . . .'.

First some definitions. The starting point, that which is accepted as given, is often called the *premiss*, or the *premisses*, for one may start with more than one proposition or piece of information as agreed. That which is claimed to follow is called the *conclusion*.

We will want to know whether conclusions are true. This will depend both on the truth of the premisses and on the soundness of the reasoning. Sound or correct reasoning is usually called *valid*. It will be the purpose of this chapter and the next to investigate what constitutes valid reasoning. It is obvious that valid reasoning from true premisses must produce true conclusions. What is not so obvious is that by incorrect reasoning we can arrive either at true or false conclusions, whatever the truth of the premisses. We can be right for the wrong reasons from true premisses as well as from false ones.

It will be simplest to make first some general points by considering particular examples. Consider the sentence: 'If X (a village) is in Yorkshire, then it is in England.'

Our knowledge of geography tells us that this is true. The area which we call Yorkshire is all completely inside the area which we call England. This fact could be checked from an atlas and could be represented by a map. To save the trouble of drawing a detailed map we propose to represent it by a diagram, thus:

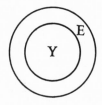

Since we know that everywhere in Yorkshire is in England, the fact that a place is in Yorkshire provides us with a *sufficient* reason for saying that it is in England, or is a *sufficient condition* for its being in England. (The word 'condition' here, and in subsequent paragraphs, is used of course in the sense of 'prerequisite' or 'qualification', and not in the sense of 'state'.)

It is obvious that in order to be in England a place doesn't *have* to be in Yorkshire. Being in Yorkshire, in other words, is not a *necessary condition* (a condition that *has* to be fulfilled), for being in England.

We can see that in order to be in Yorkshire a place must certainly be in England. Being in England, in other words, is clearly a *necessary condition* for being in Yorkshire; it is a condition that has to be fulfilled. But it is not a *sufficient* condition, the fact that a place is in England does not provide a sufficient reason for saying that it must be in Yorkshire. If we use 'Y' and 'E' to stand respectively for 'being in Yorkshire' and 'being in England', we see that the matter can be summed up thus:

Y is *sufficient* to make E true, but it is not *necessary* to make E true.

E is *necessary* to make Y true, but it is not *sufficient* to make Y true.

This result suggests that if p states a sufficient condition for q, then q states a necessary condition for p; and that if p states a necessary condition for q, then q states a sufficient condition for p. We may see clearly that this is in fact a general rule by looking at the matter from a slightly different point of view.

Suppose that a 'bohum' is defined as a red, wooden cube.

We can therefore say truly of an object: 'If it is a bohum, then it is red.' Or we could put it slightly more lengthily by saying: 'If it is red, wooden and cubical, then it is red.'

In this form the connection between necessary and sufficient conditions is clearly displayed. Obviously being red, wooden and cubical provides a sufficient reason for saying that it is red, but the condition states more than is necessary (it *need* not be wooden or cubical). And obviously being red is a necessary condition for being red, wooden and cubical, but it is not a sufficient one (it needs to be wooden and cubical as well).

Exercises

7.1. Are the conditions stated in the following sentences (a) sufficient, (b) necessary, for the conclusions?

1. If that's an ostrich, then it has two legs.
2. If it's a ripe tomato, then it's red.
3. If an animal has four legs, then it's a quadruped.
4. If a number ends in 9, then it's divisible by 3.
5. If a triangle is isosceles, then it's equilateral.
6. If it can fly, then it's a pig.
7. If it's got four wheels, then it's a motor-car.
8. If a number ends in 0, then it's divisible by 5.
9. If it's a parallelogram, then the diagonals bisect each other.
10. If it's red, wooden and cubical, then it's a bohum.
11. If p states a sufficient condition for q, then q states a necessary condition for p.

7.2. If p and q state conditions which are together sufficient for r, are they separately necessary for r? Illustrate your answer with a specific example.

7.3. p states a sufficient condition for r, r states a necessary condition for q. Can you say whether q states a sufficient or a necessary condition for p?

7.4. 1. Is a condition that is more than is sufficient, sufficient?
2. Is a condition that is more than is necessary, necessary?

It is obvious, and we hope that doing the above examples will have underlined the fact, that the conclusion only follows if the condition is sufficient. If the condition is necessary and not sufficient then the conclusion does not follow, but the *converse*, the sentence formed by exchanging the condition and the conclusion, does follow.

Consider, for example, the sentence:

'If a number is divisible by 2, then it ends in 6.'

This is not true, the condition is not sufficient. But the condition is necessary, a number must be divisible by 2 in order that it shall end in 6; or putting it in another way if it ends in 6, then it is divisible by 2. And to put it in this way is to state the converse.

We repeat this now in a general form, thus:

If p states a sufficient condition for q ('If p then q' is true), then q states a necessary condition for p ('If q, then p' need not be true).

If p states a necessary condition for q ('If p, then q' need not be true), then q states a sufficient condition for p ('If q, then p' is true).

It obviously follows that if p states a necessary and sufficient condition for q, then q states a sufficient and necessary condition for p. ('If p, then q' and 'If q, then p' are *both* true.)

In practice it will often be found that the simplest way of seeing whether p states a necessary condition for q is to think whether 'If q, then p' is true, in other words whether q states a sufficient condition for p.

If we are given 'If p, then q', and 'If q, then r' it is easy to see that we can deduce 'If p, then r'. We are told that the truth of p is sufficient to ensure the truth of q and that the truth of q is sufficient to ensure the truth of r. It follows therefore that the truth of p is sufficient to ensure the truth of q *and* r.

We consider now an example to give practice in the handling of the ideas of necessary, sufficient, etc.

'p, q, r state conditions which are separately necessary and together sufficient for x. x states a condition which is sufficient, but not necessary for y. y states a condition which is sufficient for p and necessary for z. z is true. What, if anything, can be said about the truth or falsehood of p, q, r, x, y?'

It will be simplest to set out all the facts we are given in the form 'if . . . then . . .'. Thus:

1. If p, q and r then x
2. If x then p⎫
3. If x then q⎬ (since p, q, r are separately necessary for x)
4. If x then r⎭

5. If x then y (x is sufficient for y)
6. If y then p (y is sufficient for p)
7. If z then y (y is necessary for z)

We are told that z is true. Therefore, from 7, y is true.

Therefore, from 6, p is true.

But this is as far as we can go. It is not possible to say anything about the truth or falsehood of q, r and x.

Exercises

7.5. p is sufficient for q and necessary for r; s is necessary for q and sufficient for r. Can you say whether p is sufficient and/or necessary for s?

7.6. x and y together are sufficient for p; x is necessary for q; r is sufficient for y, and necessary for s; s is sufficient for q. s is true. What can be said about the truth or falsehood of p, q, r, x, y?

7.7. If p is a necessary condition for x, then q is a sufficient condition for y; r is a sufficient condition for z; z is a necessary condition for x, and a sufficient condition for y; p is a necessary condition for y. If p is a necessary condition for q, then r is true. What, if anything, can be said about the truth or falsehood of p, q, r, x, y, z?

It will be convenient at this stage to introduce another very simple piece of notation. If p stands for a statement or proposition we sometimes want to talk about the contradictory of p, that is about not-p.

This is indicated by putting a line over the letter, thus: $\bar{p}$.

We now consider what, if anything, can be said about $\bar{p}$ and $\bar{q}$, if we know that 'If p, then q'.

Let us look again at our first example: 'If a village is in Yorkshire, then it is in England', in which the condition, though sufficient, is not necessary.

The contradictory of a village being in Yorkshire is a village not being in Yorkshire, but from this we could not deduce anything at all about whether it is in England. But the reader may already have spotted the fact that if we are told that a village is not in England we can deduce that it is not in Yorkshire.

This looks as though from 'If p, then q' we can deduce, 'If $\bar{q}$, then $\bar{p}$'. And we can in fact demonstrate this clearly without any

103

reference to the particular case of Yorkshire and England. Bearing in mind that p and p̄ are contradictories we argue as follows:

If q̄, then there are two possibilities—either p or p̄. Suppose p. Then since we took as our premiss 'If p, then q', it follows that q. But this lands us in a contradiction, for we started by saying 'If q̄'. ∴ p cannot follow from q̄.

∴ we can say that from 'If p, then q', it necessarily follows that 'if q̄, then p̄'. (This of course assumes that p and q are propositions such that p̄ and q̄ are their true contradictories, exclusive and exhaustive.)

It will be remembered that when p states a condition which is necessary as well as sufficient for q, we can also deduce from 'If p, then q' that 'If q, then p' must be true. We can then obviously go on to deduce that 'If p̄, then q̄' must also be true.

It may be useful to sum up.

When p states a condition that is sufficient, but not necessary for q:

'If p, then q'\
'If q̄, then p̄'} are true, and 'If q, then p'\
'If p̄, then q̄'} are false.

When p states a condition that is necessary, but not sufficient for q:

'If q, then p'\
'If p̄, then q̄'} are true, and 'If p then q'\
'If q̄ then p̄'} are false.

Obviously if the condition is sufficient and necessary all four of the above statements are true, and if the condition is neither sufficient nor necessary they are all false.

'ONLY IF . . .'

In any sentence of the form 'If p, then q' the claim is made that the condition is sufficient. But we cannot tell by inspection whether the condition is also claimed to be necessary. In exercise *7.1.* the reader was asked to consider whether the claim of sufficiency was justified and also whether a claim of necessity could be made, but it was only possible to do this by being acquainted with the terms involved, by knowing about ostriches, tomatoes, triangles, numbers ending in 6 and so on. It would obviously be convenient to have a form of words which will tell us briefly whether a condition is being claimed to be necessary as well as sufficient. 'If and only if . . .' provides such a form. When I say 'If and only if p, then q', I am claiming not only that p is a sufficient condition for q, but also that q cannot be true unless p is, in other words that p is also a necessary condition. This may be easier to understand if we take particular examples.

We would *not* be justified in saying: 'If and only if a number ends in 8 is it divisible by 2', or 'If and only if an animal is a cow has it got four legs', for in each case the condition is not necessary. But we clearly are justified in saying: 'If and only if a triangle has all three sides equal are all its three angles equal', for in this case the condition is necessary.

We can also use 'only if' by itself to make the claim that the condition is necessary but not sufficient. For example: 'Only if a number is even is it divisible by 6.' 'Only if he is a member will he be in the pavilion.' But there are some cases when 'only if' is used where 'if and only if' may be understood. Suppose for example that a parent says to a child 'Only if you behave yourself will I take you to the cinema this afternoon.' It is likely that the child will take this to mean that behaving himself would be a sufficient condition and not merely a necessary one for going to the cinema.

Exercises

7.8. p is necessary for the contradictory of q; the contradictory of r is necessary for q. What, if any, is the link between p and r?

7.9. The contradictory of x is sufficient for y. If p is true then y is false. The contradictory of q is necessary for x. You are told that q is true. What, if anything, can you say about p, x, y?

7.10. Express the following sentences in the form 'If ... then ...' using as few negatives as possible. State in each case whether you think the condition is likely to be necessary as well as sufficient:
1. Members only.
2. No man shall enter my house unless he has first removed his shoes.
3. Trespassers will be prosecuted.

7.11. Comment on the validity of the following arguments:
1. 'You said last year that if the cost of living index went up you would ask for an increase in wages. Since then the index has not risen by a single point, but here you are asking for an increase just the same. How do you justify your illogical behaviour?'

105

2. 'A little blonde from Munich . . . climbs the North Wall of the Eiger. So, once again, it is proved that women are as agile as men, that their nerves are as good, and their power of endurance as lasting.' (*Daily Express*)

3. If a man is an autovert, then he must be trepid; but no autovert is sanguineous. Since Clactonbirt is certainly not trepid, it follows that he is not an autovert and is sanguineous.

4. Only if a man is glibulous can he accept arquepods, and since a man can only attain becility if he accepts arquepods, it follows that all those who are glibulous are capable of attaining becility.

7.12. q necessarily follows from p, and r is a necessary condition for the contradictory of p. Only if x is true is the falsehood of q a sufficient condition for r. Is x true?

7.13. A, B, C, D, E are five quantities which have a numerical value. You are told that:
1. A is equal to C if and only if E is not equal to B.
2. Only if C is as much less than B as B is less than A, is A greater than D.
3. C is less than A and greater than D.
   What is the order of magnitude of A, B, C, D, E?

7.14. One is a noodle if and only if one is consipid and is not boolish. A necessary condition for being boolish is that one should have passed the translucency test. Anyone who has passed the translucency test is certainly not consipid. Having a name which does not begin with Q is a necessary condition for not being consipid. Can you say whether Quoodle is a noodle?

NECESSITY OF THE LINK

In the examples of 'If p, then q' that we have so far considered it has been assumed that when the condition was sufficient the conclusion followed with certainty, that it *had* to follow, that it necessarily followed. This is bound up with the fact that, as we have seen, when we claim that p is a sufficient condition for q, we also claim that q is a necessary condition for p.

For if a *necessary* qualification for p is q, then every p *must* be q. If a necessary qualification for a village to be in Yorkshire is that it must be in England, then every village in Yorkshire must necessarily be in England. If y is a condition that every x has to satisfy, then every x has to satisfy it; if x, then necessarily y.

But the nature of this necessity has been rather taken for granted. Let us examine it.

If asked to explain the necessity there might be a tendency to try to do so by repeated and emphatic assertion, 'Can't you see? It *must* be!' And in a sense this is a not unreasonable thing to do.

If I say: 'If you have an orange and an apple, then you have an orange,' then everyone would agree that the conclusion follows necessarily. It is like saying 'a rose is a rose'. The conclusion is contained in the premiss—in this case very obviously—and is merely being repeated. We who utter the sentence are not going to allow the conclusion not to follow, we make the link a necessary one. If someone says that an orange and an apple that are jointly owned become an 'orapple' and lose their separate identity we will refuse to accept it. In the sense in which we are using the words it follows necessarily that if you have an orange and an apple then you have an orange. It will be some comfort to know that almost everybody else also uses the words in such a way as to make the conclusion follow necessarily from the premiss. The important point is that this necessity does not arise from the nature of oranges and apples; nothing in the world can change it, fruit blight, earthquakes, the total destruction of the universe, nothing that can ever happen alters the fact that, in the sense in which I use the words, 'If you have an orange and an apple, then necessarily you must have an orange.'

We have taken an example where the necessity was particularly obvious. But it is important to see that in all cases where the condition is sufficient to guarantee the conclusion, where the conclusion in other words follows necessarily, the necessity is essentially of the same kind. In each case the conclusion is contained in the premises though these may not all be stated.

When I say 'If a village is in Yorkshire, then it is in England', the important premises which are not stated are the definitions of Yorkshire and England. As soon as we know what those definitions are and what it is to be 'in' we see that the conclusion is contained in the premises and is merely being specifically stated. Suppose I say 'If it's a ripe tomato, then it's red'. It may well be that everyone would not agree with this, that someone might claim to have found a ripe tomato that was not red. This draws attention to the fact that it is only true, that the condition is only sufficient, if part of our definition of a ripe tomato is that it should be red. The conclusion in other words only follows necessarily if we put the necessity in.

The reader will have realised that we are making again about sentences of the form 'If ... then ...' a point that we have previously made about analytic or agreement statements. These, it will be remembered, are statements of definition or describe agreements and, if true, they are necessarily so; they are made true. The world of everyday events, the contingent world, is not allowed to interfere with them. The system that is being dealt with is a closed system, shut off from the world outside.

Just as analytic statements are made true, and the necessity is put in, so conclusions which follow necessarily from premises can only do so if they are already there; they follow necessarily because we who constructed the premises put them in there, perhaps without being aware of it, and are now drawing them out.

This process of drawing out conclusions from premises is often called *deduction*. It is also described as arguing from the general to the particular, and is contrasted with *induction*, which is more nearly a process of arguing from the particular to the general.

DEDUCTION

The processes of deduction which we have considered so far have been very obvious ones. It was really hardly necessary to point out that from the premiss: 'It is red, wooden and cubical' we can deduce that it is red. But we have made the examples obvious in order to exhibit in skeleton form the structure of what is happening when one deduces.

We consider now some more cases.

If $A >$ (is greater than) B,
then $B <$ (is less than) A.

Most people become acquainted with these symbols, and this piece of deduction, from the study of mathematics when A and B are numbers or lengths or angles. As soon as we understand what it is to be greater than, we see that the fact of A being greater than B involves and includes B being less than A. It is merely another way of stating the same fact. It follows necessarily because it's already there.

We may now go on to say:

If $A > B$ and $B > C$, then $A > C$

Again once we understand the nature of being greater than, we see that it follows necessarily, the conclusion is contained in, involved by the premises.

But we note that the idea of 'greater than' can only be applied to certain things and exactly what is meant by it may require careful definition. If A, B and C stand for numbers, there is no difficulty, but the remark 'This table is greater than this chair' would be so ambiguous as to be meaningless without further clarification. Does it mean that the table is heavier, taller, more expensive, more important, some combination of these or something quite different? We note also that we must compare like with like. When we say: 'If $A > B$ and $B > C$' no conclusion follows unless the two signs $>$ both mean greater than in exactly the same respect. In other words, it is only a necessary conclusion if it is applied to the sort of things to which it can be applied, and if it is applied in such a way as to make it necessarily true.

One of the best known examples of a complicated deductive system is that of Euclidean Geometry. In this case the conclusions that are produced are certainly not contained obviously in the original premises or axioms—or perhaps we should say that anyone who finds them obvious is a very clever person indeed. And it may seem rather hard in such a case to justify a claim that what is deduced is in some sense already there. The best way to be convinced is to go through a complicated proof step by step, to examine microscopically the links in the chain as though we were having to explain it to someone who was being very obstinate or stupid, and we will see that each small step is necessitated by, is contained in, the position that has been reached before that step is taken. If it is not so necessitated, one is not justified in taking the step. In order to see that it follows necessarily we must understand the nature of what it is that we are talking about. We can only see that if $A > B$ and $B > C$, then A is not equal to C, if we understand what it means to be greater and to be equal.

The reader will already have examined and constructed such

109

chains of argument if he has attempted the closed system exercises in Chapter 1. In each case the conclusion was contained in what was given. It must have been; where else could it have come from? Though it is true of course that in addition to the premisses that were stated, other unstated premisses were often taken for granted and used—for example that 'either it is or it isn't' was applicable to various statements and characteristics.

SUMMARY. See p. 120

Chapter 8

The Structure of Reasoning–2

ALTERNATIVE WAYS OF SAYING 'IF...THEN...'

1. As the reader has probably already realised, an alternative way of expressing the fact 'If a village is in Yorkshire, then it is in England' would be to say 'All Yorkshire villages are in England'. This was obvious from the diagram we used on p. 95. We could clearly have said here 'All Y's are E's'.

When we use the 'if... then...' form we do not say whether being in Yorkshire is a necessary as well as a sufficient condition for being in England; in the other form we do not say whether all E's are Y's. In fact we know from our knowledge of Yorkshire and England that the condition is not necessary and that all E's are not Y's.

It is obvious that if the condition were sufficient *and* necessary we could say 'all Y's are E's and all E's are Y's' and we could represent the matter in a diagram thus:

2. Another alternative follows from seeing that 'if p, then q' implies that p cannot be associated with not-q. If we know that all A's are B's, then we also know that we cannot have an A which is not a B.

'*Not both p and q̄*' *is therefore equivalent to* '*If p, then q*'.

It is not a form which is used very often. Examples are: 'You can't have an isosceles △ which doesn't have its angles equal.' 'You can't have it both ways.'

3. The next alternative is best explained by considering an example:

A notice might go up: 'All boys must wear either a tie or a jacket or both.'

It will be seen that if a boy is wearing a tie he may, but need not, wear a jacket. But if he is not wearing a tie he *must* wear a jacket. He must wear at least one of the two articles, tie and jacket.

We can see from this that '*Either p or q or both*' *is equivalent to* '*If p̄, then q*', or (which amounts to the same thing), 'if q̄, then p'.

If we then want to find the corresponding equivalent for 'If p, then q', in 'either ... or ...' terms, we must clearly in the above equivalence substitute p for p̄, and therefore also p̄ for p.

Just as 'If p̄, then q', is equivalent to 'Either p or q or both', so 'If p, then q' will be equivalent to 'Either p̄ or q or both'. Most people do not find the equivalence so obvious when it is put this way round and it may help to look at the example with a tie and a jacket again.

Suppose the notice said: 'Every boy must be tieless (p̄) or wear a jacket (q), or both.'

In this case a boy may be tieless with no jacket, or tieless with one, but if he *does* wear a tie he must also wear a jacket. The combination which is not allowed is for him to be neither tieless nor jacketed. 'Either tieless or jacketed or both' is therefore seen to be equivalent to 'If a tie, then a jacket'.

EQUIVALENCE FURTHER EXPLAINED

Another way of exhibiting the equivalence of these alternatives is as follows.

As far as the truth of p and q is concerned there are four possibilities:

1. p, q   3. p̄, q
2. p, q̄   4. p̄, q̄

When we say 'If p, then q' we exclude possibility 2. We do not in fact say anything about the possibilities, 'If p̄', but there is no implication that either 3 or 4 is excluded.

When we say 'Not both p and q̄', we even more obviously exclude 2 and allow the possibility of the other three.

We can see that 'Either p̄ or q or both' again specifically excludes 2, which is neither p̄ nor q, but allows 1, 3 and 4 where either p̄ or q or both are true.

Exercise 8.1
Arrange the following sentences in equivalent groups:
1. If q̄, then p̄.
2. Either p or q̄ or both.
3. Not both p and q.
4. Either q or p or both.
5. If p̄, then q.
6. If q, then p̄.
7. Not both q and p̄.
8. If q̄, then p.
9. Either p̄ or q or both.
10. Not both p and q̄.
11. If p, then q.
12. If q, then p.
13. Either p̄ or q̄ or both.
14. If p, then q̄.
15. Not both q̄ and p̄.
16. If p̄ then q̄.

Let us consider now how best to tackle a fairly complicated deductive problem based on the principles we have just been studying.

'Either x is false or y is true or both. Only if y is false can z be true. It is not possible both for p to be true and z to be false. If p is false, then q is false too. But q is not false. What can be said about the truth or falsehood of p, x, y, z?'

We first put all the information in the 'if ... then ...' form, in order that we may more easily see how the different items may be linked up.

'Either x̄ or y or both' becomes 'If x, then y'	1.
'Only if ȳ, z' becomes 'If z, then ȳ'	2.
'Not both p and z̄' becomes 'If p, then z'	3.
and we also have 'If p̄, then q̄'	4.

Since we are told that q is true we start with 4, which we know can be written 'If q, then p'.

Since q is true, therefore p is true. And from 3, therefore z is true. And from 2, therefore y is false. We now write 1 as 'If ȳ, then x̄', and we see that since y is false, x is also false.

Therefore p and z are true; x and y are false.

In tackling examples in which the classes have names it will be easiest to use letters as abbreviations when setting out the data.

The reader should by now be clear about the five main forms which are equivalent to each other, namely:

All p's are q's.

If p, then q.

If q̄, then p̄.

Not both p and q̄.

Either p̄ or q or both.

To find the forms which are equivalent to 'If p, then q̄' we substitute q̄ for q, and q for q̄ in the above; and similarly for other examples.

It will usually be found simplest to put all the data in the form 'If... then...', and the reader is particularly warned to remember that 'If q, then p' can *not* be deduced from, is *not* equivalent to, 'If p, then q', unless we are told that p provides a necessary as well as a sufficient condition for q.

Exercises

8.2. You are told that all dogs bark. Which of the following are therefore true?

1. If it barks then it's a dog.
2. Either it doesn't bark or it's not a dog or both.
3. If it's not a dog then it doesn't bark.
4. It can't both not bark and be a dog.
5. If it doesn't bark then it's not a dog.
6. Either it's a dog or it doesn't bark or both.

8.3. If x is true then y is false. Either y is true or z is false or both. z is false if and only if p is false. But p is true. What can you say about y, x and z?

8.4. The falsehood of p is necessary for the falsehood of q. Either r is true or s is false or both. Not both p and r. You are told that p is true. What can you say about q, r, and s?

8.5. If a man is over forty he cannot be a member of Yeovil Youngsters. Everyone of importance in Somerset is either a member of Yeovil Youngsters or of Ilchester Idlers or both. Only if one is allowed to enter the Taunton Temple of Torpor can one be a member of Ilchester Idlers. You cannot both not be under thirty and be allowed to enter the Taunton Temple of Torpor.

Smith is someone of importance in Somerset and is not under thirty. What else can you say about him?

8.6. If p is a necessary condition for q, then either r is true or s is false or both. The contradictory of q is a necessary condition for the contradictory of r. r cannot be true if p is false. If s is true, what can be said about the truth or falsehood of p, q, r?

8.7. The following notice goes up:

Clothing Regulations

(1) Only if a boy is over 16 may he wear a tail coat.
(2) No boy who is not over 15 may wear a top hat.
(3) The wearing of either a top hat or a tail coat or both is a necessary condition for watching cricket on Saturday afternoon.
(4) If a boy is either carrying an umbrella or over 16 or both he may not wear a jubilee jersey.
(5) Boys must either not watch cricket or wear a jubilee jersey or both.

What can you say about the age and apparel of those watching cricket on Saturday afternoon?

8.8. 'I have been studying the regulations for entry into the island of Utopia. They say that those who are over fifty and have never done any manual work will be allowed in unless they either suffer from verbosia or have never been trunculated or both. No one over forty in our village has both had verbosia and been trunculated. And if anyone has not been trunculated, well then of course he must have been a manual worker. It seems to me that as I'm fifty-five and have never done a stroke of manual work they're bound to let me in all right.'

Do you agree? Justify your answer.

THE SYLLOGISM

A particular form of argument whereby, from the combination of two premisses a conclusion is deduced, is called a *syllogism*.

An example is:

'All qualified scientists are clear thinkers;
Robinson is a qualified scientist;
∴. Robinson is a clear thinker.'

We will not for the moment consider whether 'qualified scientists' and 'clear thinkers' are clearcut categories or whether the two premisses are true. If, however, we grant their truth it is obvious that the conclusion follows. As a matter of interest the argument could equally well have been put in the 'If ... then ... ' form which we have recently been considering. Thus:

If a man is a qualified scientist, then he's a clear thinker; if it's Robinson then he's a qualified scientist; but it is Robinson ... etc.

In the syllogistic form of the argument the first two lines are called the Major and Minor Premiss respectively and the last line the conclusion. Since from the combination of the two premisses a conclusion is derived, they must have some item in common; in the example we have given the common item, which occurs in both the premisses, is 'qualified scientists'. This is called the *Middle Term*; it mediates between, or connects up, the other two terms, 'clear thinkers' and 'Robinson'. Notice that this middle or mediating term has no place in the conclusion.

Traditionally the two premisses and the conclusion of a syllogism were always in the form 'All or some A's are or are not B's,' and it used to be thought that all argument could be reduced to a series of syllogisms. It is agreed now that it is not sensible to try to do this, and that the attempt is bound to result in an unnatural twisting and misrepresentation of the things we want to say and the ways in which we want to argue. It will not therefore be profitable for us here to go into details about the conventions of the syllogism, and the principles that can be laid down about which combinations are valid—that is, produce conclusions that truly follow from the premisses and are therefore true if they are.

We shall content ourselves with pointing out one particular type of syllogism which is not valid, and we shall then give the reader a variety of examples, where he can use his intelligence to decide whether or not valid syllogisms are formed.

Consider the following:

'Some A's are B's.   Some A's are C's.   ∴. Some C's are B's.'

It should be obvious that the conclusion here does not follow, and it is easy to see why. We have seen that the middle term mediates between or connects up the other two items or terms mentioned in the premises (in this case B's and C's). But in this example, although the middle term, 'Some A's', appears to be the same in both premises it could easily refer to a completely different group, a different collection of A's, on the two occasions. This can be seen even more obviously if we say:

'Some schoolmasters are over forty.   Some schoolmasters are under thirty.'

It is quite clear that no conclusion can be drawn. 'Some schoolmasters' is not here a genuine middle term, it refers to different groups of people.

An important conclusion we can come to therefore is that on at least one of the occasions on which it is used the middle term must refer to *all* the members of the class; if the reference is only to some on both occasions no conclusion can be drawn.

If we were to say for example: 'All the masters in this school are over forty. Some of the masters in this school are tennis players', we could draw the valid conclusion that some schoolmasters over forty are tennis players.

8.9. Does the conclusion follow from the premises in the following syllogisms? If not, explain clearly why not.
1. Some A's are not B's.   No B's are C's.   ∴. Some C's are not A's.
2. All bishops are devout.   Some clergymen are not bishops.   ∴. Some clergymen are not devout.
3. Some A's are B's.   All C's are A's.   ∴. Some C's are B's.
4. No B's are C's.   No A's are B's.   ∴. No A's are C's.
5. Some Socialists are not intelligent.   All Socialists are idealists. ∴. Some idealists are not intelligent.
6. All Conservatives are warm hearted.   All Conservatives are realists.   ∴. Some realists are warm hearted.

117

8.10. 'Indeed, it seems to me that you can derive the original behaviourist doctrine from a kind of distorted syllogism: all physicists are scientists; no physicist talks to the things he is studying; therefore no scientist talks to the things he is studying.' (MAX HAMMERTON, 'Down with Philosophy!' *The Listener*)

Is this syllogism valid? If not, what change in the premisses would be necessary to make the conclusion follow?

8.11. What conclusion, if any, can be deduced from the following sets of premisses?
1. No A's are B's. Some C's are B's.
2. Some Europeans are snail-eaters. All Italians are Europeans.
3. Some stupid people are not wicked. No Liberals are stupid.
4. All P's are Q's. Some A's are not P's.
5. Some smokers die young. Some Irishmen are smokers.

DIFFERENT PURPOSES OF 'IF ... THEN ...'

In these two chapters we have been considering the structure of logical argument, the machinery of 'If ... then ...' and equivalent sentences, and how they can be combined to produce valid conclusions.

The reader may have noticed that some of our uses of 'If ... then ...' in the exercises have not, strictly speaking, been cases of logical deduction. And it is important to realise that these logical argument sentences are used for other purposes which though similar in many respects are yet significantly different.

RULES AND REGULATIONS

In Exercise *8.7*, for example, 'If ... then ...', 'Either ... or ...' etc. were used, as they very frequently are, to lay down regulations. One is not saying here, as a matter of logic, that if $A > B$ then it *must* follow that $B < A$. One is saying that if a boy is under fifteen he *must* not wear a top hat. The 'must' is clearly different in kind. In the first case it is a 'must' of necessarily following and if we are arguing correctly there will be no exceptions, we are not allowing any. But in the second case the 'must' is an order. We might say again that we are not allowing any exceptions, and we may try very hard not to, but we know perfectly well that exceptions are possible, that rules and regulations frequently are broken in a way in which logical rules cannot be. And the reason, of course, is that we are dealing with the open system world of people wearing or not wearing top hats, instead of the closed system world of logical necessity.

But although rules and regulations do not carry the same kind of necessity, nevertheless, as we saw when doing the exercises, the 'Either... or...' etc. sentences which refer to them can be combined in the same way and according to the same principles. The 'conclusions' which will follow will then have the same sort of strength as the premisses; there will be a 'must' which entails that this is what is ordered, what ought to be done, with the implication perhaps that if it isn't punishment will follow.

And it is interesting, as those who have done Exercise 8.7 may have realised, that we are probably more familiar with the 'Either ...or...' and the 'Not both...and...' forms of 'If...then...' and find them easier to understand, in their rules and regulations uses than in their strictly lógical uses. If I say 'Either you take your hat off or you won't be allowed in', you are unlikely to need a pause for reflecting what you should do with your hat if you want to get in. But if I say 'Either it's not an erkwill or it's got two legs', you might have to think for a moment before deciding whether an erkwill has got two legs or not.

CAUSE AND EFFECT

But the most frequent of all the uses of 'If ... then ...' is to state a causal connection, perhaps to make a prediction. 'If I let go of this, it will fall to the ground' (the 'then' is usually omitted); 'If you try to run a mile in less than five minutes, you will fail'; 'If you don't put any petrol in the car you can hardly expect it to go.'

Or we may make a statement about the past, a judgment about what would have happened *if* things had been different: 'If Jones had been able to come to the party, I'm sure he would have enjoyed himself.'

Such uses are obviously about an open system and there is no question here of logical necessity. Often in making them we may insert some remark about how certain or likely we think the predicted consequence is. But we are bound to admit that we may be wrong, though often we may never discover this. Clearly when we make a judgment about what would have happened if things had been different in the past we can never know whether we are right, our judgment is not capable of verification.

We shall try in the next chapter to examine the nature of the causal link, what it is that justifies us in claiming a conclusion, even though only a tentative one. And we shall examine in more detail the whole structure of open system argument.

Exercise 8.12
Consider whether the links in the following sentences are (a) *logical* (and therefore by definition necessary), or (b) *regulative* (i.e. laid down by regulation and therefore necessary in a different and less strict sense): or (c) *causal* (and therefore not necessary, but more or less certain), or some combination of these:
1. You must either get your hair cut or stay away from my lectures.
2. If you don't let go of that you'll get an electric shock.
3. If we have another period of inflation, the result must be a rise in the cost of living.
4. Either Blugg is telling the truth or he is not.
5. If you drive carelessly you are likely to have an accident.
6. 'B.O.A.C. must be run as a commercial undertaking. If it is to make ends meet, remain one of the great airlines of the world, and be absolutely competitive, it must buy its aeroplanes wherever it most advantageously can.' *The Times*.
7. 'We can either enjoy a stable monetary framework but suffer from economic inefficiencies, or we can enjoy a more efficient allocation of labour but suffer from inflation.' (Letter to *The Times*)

8. For public exhibition to adult audiences only.

SUMMARY OF CHAPTERS 7 and 8
1. *Sufficient* and *necessary* conditions and how they fit in with 'if . . . then . . .' are summed up on p. 99.
2. 'Only if' is a way of stating that the condition is necessary, but not sufficient. It may not, however, always be understood in this way.
3. The logical link is *necessary*, because it merely *draws out* what was already in the premisses. Hence the word *Deduction*.
4. Alternative ways of saying 'If . . . then . . .' are summed up on p. 109.
5. The syllogism is a form of argument to which too much importance has sometimes been attached in the past. It is not sensible to

try to put all our reasoning in syllogistic form. Nevertheless it is useful to know what a syllogism is and to have some practice in dealing with them and assessing their validity.

6. 'If ... then . .' and its equivalents are used not only for logical deduction but also to lay down regulations and to describe or predict causes and effects. The structure of the reasoning is the same, but the necessity or certainty are different.

Chapter 9

Open System Thinking

We have mentioned in previous chapters that our most important thinking is about the world around us, what we have called open system thinking. It is obviously desirable that we should try to make this thinking better, clearer, more effective. In order to understand more fully what we mean by this and how to achieve it we consider now what our open system thinking is *for*, we take a look at a few basic principles.

As men grow up and develop they find that they want to achieve certain ends, to satisfy their needs and desires. These needs in the first place were what we should now call elementary or primitive. Our primitive ancestors wanted, like animals, to satisfy their hunger and thirst, to protect themselves from heat and cold and rain, and from the attacks of other animals or men. As time went on and man, or some men, succeeded in satisfying these simple needs their wants became more refined, more complicated, more advanced. Greater comfort, bigger and better dwelling places, more efficient and more rapid methods of moving about the surface of the earth, art, literature, music: these are some of the things which civilised man now enjoys.

In order to achieve these things in the past man has had to learn to *control* his environment. In order to control it he has had to understand how it works, he has had to be able to explain why certain things have happened, and he has had to be able to predict at least to some extent what will happen in the future.

In order to understand, predict, control, man has had to use his mind and think. Clear and effective thinking in this context is that which produces the most desirable (or the most *desired*) result in the most economical way, that is with the least expenditure of human effort. There is no doubt about what clear thinking is *for* in this context, it is for the most efficient and effective accomplishment of our heart's desires.

ENDS AND MEANS

It is often said that our ends, the things at which we aim, are dictated by our feelings, our desires; but that our means, the methods we use to achieve these ends, are devised by our minds. That is what the philosopher David Hume meant when he said: 'Reason is and ought only to be the slave of the passions.' What one wanted was decided by the emotions or the passions, how one was to get it was decided by the reason. The picture is of the passions deciding 'I want that apple at the top of the tree', and commanding the reason to work out a method of getting it.

But this way of looking at it involves a dangerous over-simplification. The analogy of a tyrant indulging his slightest whim breaks down when the passions and the reason belong to the same person, who not only has to devise the method but also to carry it out. It is the mouth of Bloggs that waters as he sees the apple, it is the mind of Bloggs that reckons that a ladder placed there and stretching up to there will do the job; but if it is also the body of Bloggs that will have to stagger under the weight of the ladder, and the life of Bloggs that will be hazarded, then Bloggs is likely to think again.

Think again. Notice that the reason will be employed not merely to devise means for achieving ends, but to decide on the merits of the end, whether it is desirable or not. And this brings us, of course, to the very important point that means and ends are to a considerable extent relative terms. The apple is desired, in a sense, as an end; but it might also be said that it is desired as a means of satisfying Bloggs's appetite, of giving him pleasure. When Bloggs thinks again he may decide that the dissatisfaction involved in fetching the ladder and climbing it will outweigh the satisfaction he would get from eating the apple.

The balancing of the desirability of ends, especially of longer-term ends, is one of the most important functions of reason and one of the main distinguishing marks of a civilised man. A very primitive man, like some animals, tends to live from day to day or almost from moment to moment. As he becomes conscious of wanting or needing something, reason may be employed immediately in devising means for satisfying that want as soon as possible, with little or no thought of longer-term wants.

But as man becomes more civilised, or in order to become more civilised, he learns the desirability of postponing present satisfaction in order to secure greater satisfaction in the future. In order to build a better house we must go without some of the things that we would like to have *now*, some of the short-term ends that we would like to achieve; we will do this because we think that in the long run, taking all things into consideration, we shall be happier. If our ancestors had never looked ahead, had thought only of their own immediate short-term advantage, life today would clearly be very different. We may not always approve of the judgments that were made in the past about the balance of advantage, but without a great deal of thinking about the comparative desirability of short- and long-term ends there can be no progress.

The assessment that is required in order to balance the claims of competing ends is far from easy, though it is a matter usually for imagination and delicate judgment rather than for great intelligence and thinking power. It is interesting that on the whole we associate stupidity with lack of foresight, with preferring short-term to long-term goals, whereas we think that the more intelligent man will put money aside for his old age rather than spend it all now. It is often the case too that to look ahead, to prefer long-term, more lasting advantages for oneself and the community is associated with a higher moral standard. A man may refrain from telling a lie for short-term personal gain because he has been told that it is wrong to do so, but he may also refrain because he has the intelligence and the imagination to see that the long-term advantage of being a person whose word is believed is likely to outweigh any short-term advantage that may result from the lie.

We see then that this balancing of ends is largely a matter of assessing their comparative desirability, of deciding where we want to go. But it is obviously also important to know how to set about getting there and to have some idea of how likely we are to succeed. To this end we must be able to understand the world in which we live, to make predictions about it, to some extent to control it. We consider first the question of understanding it.

UNDERSTANDING THE WORLD

All our knowledge of the world comes to us through our senses. We see and hear and smell and taste and touch. And by looking, reading and listening we learn about the experiences of other people. The experience of our senses does not present itself in a very orderly

125

fashion and the human mind by observing regularities, by classifying experiences which resemble each other in some way, imposes order on the chaos. We have already seen in Chapter 3 how necessary the process of classification is for a great deal of our thinking. We observe characteristics which are found together, we note that all animals which fly have legs, and we make a generalisation about it and formulate a law or a principle. We would have to admit when we make such a generalisation that we may be wrong, that an exception may be found. But quite often we couch the generalisation in such a way as not to allow exceptions, we make it an analytic statement, or a matter of definition. The entomologist can quite easily ensure that there are no exceptions to the generalisation 'All lepidoptera have four membranous scale-covered wings' by making the possession of such wings a necessary qualification for membership of 'lepidoptera'.

In our observations of the world around us we notice characteristics which are frequently or usually found together—that Chinamen have yellow skins, that dogs have the capacity to bark, that human beings have two legs, that ravens are black, and so on. We also notice that certain events or types of event habitually follow each other, that if pins are inserted into balloons there is a loud pop, that if pens are applied to paper marks are made, that if ice is placed in the sun it becomes water.

As a result of our observations and experience we form generalisations—dogs bark, balloons burst if pricked. These are sometimes called *empirical* generalisations (empirical=derived from experience), and the process of forming them is called *induction*. As we mentioned in the last chapter this is the process of arguing from the particular to the general, of deriving a general conclusion from many particular cases. Unless, as in the example of the lepidoptera, we make it a matter of definition, we cannot get certainty from the inductive process, though we may get a high degree of probability. From the deductive process, however, where we are drawing out what is in the premisses we get certainty or necessity.

When the pricking of the balloon is followed by a pop we say that the one event *causes* the other. We say this because we have grown up with the idea of causation, but we may not be very clear about what it is to cause or the nature of the connection. When we say that we want to understand the world it will on the whole be causal connections that we will seek to investigate. We will ask questions, and we will expect answers of a kind that will explain to us what was not previously clear. Let us consider the questions that we will ask and the sort of answers that will count as explanations, that will satisfy us.

If we are seeking understanding rather than knowledge the questions that we ask will on the whole be prefaced by 'Why' or 'How'. At an obvious mechanical level we might ask 'How does that machine work?' or, if it has gone wrong, 'Why is that machine not working?' There would normally be no doubt about the kind of answer that is expected. We should expect to have traced for us a mechanical chain of causes and effects. The amount of detail that we would require in order to be satisfied that we understand would depend on how well acquainted we were with that sort of machine. Modern man would need little or no explanation of how a bicycle works; primitive man might have required a great deal. It is important to notice that any further or more detailed explanation can only consist of supplying more links in the causal chain. I might be told that the bicycle is made to move forward by the pressure of one's foot on the pedal, but I might still not see exactly how or why that happens. It might then be explained to me how the chain works and causes the rear wheel to go round, but perhaps I don't understand why the whole bicycle should go forward just because the rear wheel goes round. I should then have to be told about the action of friction. But however many links are put in to make the explanation more complete, I might still, obstinately or stupidly, refuse to be satisfied, continue to ask why and how. What answer would you make if I say 'I don't see why, just because you press this thing it should move'?

In the last resort, although with the increase of scientific knowledge we can now fill in many more links in mechanical processes than we could, the answer is bound to be 'It just does. That is the way things are. Look around you and see.' At the level at which we are now considering things we must take this causal link for granted in general as a fact of experience, though in particular cases we may of course want to scrutinise the facts very carefully to see whether we are satisfied that it is there. Before we come to consider just what evidence is needed in practice to entitle us to say 'because', that 'A *causes B*', there are one or two other points that need to be made.

127

WHY?

An important difference between two types of 'Why' questions is well illustrated by the following passage from G. K. Chesterton in which he is describing a master at St Paul's School:

> 'Why are boys sent to school, Robinson?' 'To learn, sir.' 'No, boy, no; it was because one day at breakfast Mr Robinson said to Mrs Robinson, "My dear, we must do something about that boy. He's a nuisance to me and a nuisance to you, and he's a perfect plague to the servants.' Then with an indescribable extreme of grinding and grating contempt, ' "So we'll pay some man" '. . .[1]

The answer that Robinson gives is in terms of purpose, what boys are sent to school *for*. The answer that the master gives is in terms of the previous events which *caused* Robinson to go to school in the same sort of way as pressing a switch causes a light to come on. A cause which describes a purpose is usually called a *final* cause (the sentences describing it will often start 'in order to'); the other type is usually called an *efficient* or a *mechanical* cause. As we see from the above extract the answer to a 'Why' question may be quite different according to the type of cause that the questioner is assumed to be seeking.

When we enquire why some merely mechanical or physical event happened or failed to happen, for example 'Why won't the car go?', or 'Why did that bridge collapse?' we are likely to expect an answer in terms of efficient causes. We ascribe purpose only to living things and we do not suppose that a bridge collapses *in order to* fulfil some purpose, although of course it is perfectly possible for people to take steps to make it collapse *in order to* prevent the enemy crossing it.

When a 'Why' question is asked about some person's action the answer may be in terms either of a final or of an efficient cause or sometimes both. The question 'Why are you wearing that frock?' might be answered by 'In order to keep cool', or 'Because it's the only one I've got.' Sometimes the person questioned may deliberately misunderstand what it is that the questioner wants to know and give a foolishly facetious answer of the wrong kind. To the question 'Why are these books on the table?' the answer 'Because

[1] Quoted by H. Heckstall-Smith: *Doubtful School-Master* (Peter Davies), p. 182.

they were put there' is not likely to be a satisfying one. The questioner probably wants to know for what purpose they were put there. Another type of facetious, unsatisfying answer may be of the right or expected kind but may give an efficient cause that is too proximate, too near to the event that is being investigated. If someone asks, for example, 'Why did those two cars collide?', the answer 'Because they were at the same place at the same time', is unlikely to be considered satisfactory. The questioner is clearly in search of causes which are rather further back in the chain.

Exercise 9.1
Consider which type of answer (final or efficient) is more likely to be required to the following questions. If possible, suggest an answer of each type:

1. Why did you fall down?	6. Why have prices risen?
2. Why are you taking this examination?	7. Why did that aeroplane crash?
	8. Why is the toast burnt?
3. Why have the lights gone out?	9. Why do snails have shells?
4. Why are you late?	10. Why did you park your car there?
5. Why aren't you wearing a hat?	

In considering the last exercise the reader may have come to the conclusion—perfectly correctly—that in some cases, in a close analysis, the distinction between a final and an efficient cause may be difficult to uphold. If I am asked why I ate that bun, I might reply either 'Because I was hungry', or 'In order to satisfy my hunger'. The first answer appears to give an efficient cause, my action followed as a result of my feelings. The second answer appears to give a final cause, my action was in pursuit of a purpose. But it is clear that to act in pursuit of a purpose is the same thing as to act as a result of one's feelings. The modern tendency to take a greater interest in psychological motivation leads us to see that the distinction between the two kinds of causes is inevitably blurred; for whenever one acts for a purpose, in order to achieve something, one is necessarily at the same time acting as a result of one's psychological state. But in spite of the fact that the two types of cause seem to merge into one on a close examination, nevertheless the distinction is often a useful one to make. 'Because my watch stopped' and 'in order to annoy' are in important respects different kinds of reasons for being late and it is helpful to our thinking to see them as such.

We must not lose sight of the fact that all questions are asked in a particular context. 'Why' requires an explanation, but the questioner may not always be very clear as to what sort of explanation he expects and wants. We also note that an explanation that satisfies some people may be far from satisfactory to others. Answers as to why something has happened may merely describe the event in other words, and therefore say nothing to describe the cause. To the question, for example, 'Why have prices risen?' the answer might be given 'Because the value of money has fallen'. This tells us nothing about the chain of events that has caused prices to rise for a fall in the value of money is exactly the same thing, looked at from a different point of view, as a general rise in prices. It would not be very sensible of anybody to be satisfied by such an answer. It is as though to the question 'Why is A above B?' the answer was given 'Because B is below A'.

When someone asks 'Why?' in search of an efficient cause, he can hardly expect a description of the whole causal chain, for this would clearly be impossible. We have seen that the immediately antecedent cause may sometimes be just facetious and unhelpful. In general he is likely to want to know the main or significant items, but there may be differences of opinion as to which these are. It is not possible to generalise or to be definite about what counts as a satisfactory explanation. On the whole we can merely consider what sort of explanation would satisfy us, what we would be likely to want to know if we asked that question.

Exercise 9.2

Do the answers given to the following questions seem to you to be satisfactory explanations? If not, why not? Discuss, and where appropriate suggest alternatives.

1. Why are you looking so smart?   Because I've put on my best suit.
2. Why did you try to climb Mount Everest?   Because it was there.
3. Why does opium send people to sleep?   Because of its dormitive properties.
4. Why did you save so little last year?   Because I spent so much.
5. Why are you so sleepy?   Because I'm tired.

6. Why is tobacco more expensive now? Because the manufacturers have put the price up.

7. Why did you move your Bishop there? In order to threaten his Queen.

HOW?

'How' questions—apart from the conventional 'How are you?'— are normally requests for detailed descriptions of chains of events, very often causal ones. If I ask 'How does that machine work?' it is because I do not understand the mechanical processes and want them explained to me. If I ask 'How did you come here?' I probably want to know whether you came by train, by car or by bicycle; or perhaps I may want information about your route. The man who asks 'How did you do that?' wants to have details of the method explained to him. Often a 'how' question may be nearly the same as a 'why' question. 'How did the toast get burnt?' will probably receive the same sort of answer as 'Why is the toast burnt?', except that it is possible, though not very likely, that the appropriate answer to the second question, but not to the first, might be 'Because John likes his toast burnt'. On the whole a 'why' question is likely to expect an answer further back in the causal chain; perhaps the cause that is thought to be particularly important. Whereas the 'how' question expects a more general description of causes and effects. I have just heard it stated on the wireless '*How* a hurricane is formed is known, but not *why*.' I take this to mean that a detailed description can be given of the events which follow each other in the building up of a hurricane, but that this chain cannot be taken further back; it is not known exactly what makes it start.

CAUSAL CHAINS

But whether we ask 'How' or 'Why', it is, as we have already remarked, chains of causes and effects that we want to know about in order to understand the world. We may be looking for the causes of known effects, as when teams of research workers investigate the causes of cancer, or when economists try to find out why prices have risen. And in making these investigations steps will be taken to discover the effects of various actions, what happens to rats if they are given a certain course of treatment. Or we may try to discover the links in what we have strong reason to suppose is a

131

causal chain. We plant a seed and later, in the same place, a lettuce appears. What happened in between?

There seems to be no doubt that the way in which we form the idea that events are connected by what we have come to call a causal link is by observing regularities in the world around us. The infant discovers that pressure applied to a rattle is followed by the rattle moving, and in fact the infant in its pram finds out a large number of principles, of events which seem invariably to follow each other. More knowledge and sophistication is required in order to formulate these principles, but a natural curiosity and a common-sense method of trial and error may be sufficient to discover them. From our observation of nature we find out quite early on in our lives, though we are unlikely to express this in words, that the same set of circumstances or happenings will always be followed by the same event; that if we squeeze that toy there will be a squeak; that if we pull *this* string it will move, but if we pull *that* one it won't. It doesn't on the whole seem to be the case that we need any-one to tell us about the regularity of nature in this respect; we dis-cover it by observation and experience. But we also discover how very often the circumstances are not the same, that the door that opened yesterday won't open today, that the toy that has squeaked for all these weeks has ceased to do so. But I wonder whether any-one can remember a time when as a result of happenings of this kind he has ceased to believe in the uniformity of nature, the operation of causal links. Our reaction would always be not to doubt that causes operate but to discover how the circumstances are different. *Why* won't the door open? Is it locked or jammed? What's gone wrong with the toy that it won't squeak any more?

We take the causal link for granted. Let us consider now rather more strictly and formally how we investigate whether it exists in particular cases. If we want to know whether A causes B we try to find out whether A is invariably followed by B, provided that nothing else intervenes. If A stands for 'letting go of my pen' and B for 'its downward movement' the experiment would not be a difficult one to make and to repeat. We know the sort of things that must not be allowed to intervene because it has not been difficult to discover the ways in which simple events like letting go of objects, their movements and their ceasing to move, habitually fol-low each other. If A stands for events or circumstances that can be enacted or reproduced in a scientific laboratory, for example the mixing of chemicals, the workings of some machine, the experiment will not in principle be difficult; it should be easy to make the events the same or very nearly the same, and to prevent other events intervening, which amounts to the same thing. But the more complex A is and the less it is possible to perform the experiment in a laboratory and prevent other events from intervening, the harder it will be to say that A is always followed by B, that A causes B. If we want to know, for example, whether an increase in the standard rate of income tax will cause prices to fall, any investigations we make will obviously be very inconclusive. Even if we have the power to make the experiment once, we can never make it again in anything like exactly the same conditions, for the economy is changing the whole time in innumerable ways. To assert that since on a particular occasion an increase in income tax was followed by a fall in prices and therefore the one caused the other would be rash indeed. It would be rather like the primitive savage who noted that the only eclipse of the sun he had experienced was followed by his having a violent toothache and came to the conclusion that the one event caused the other.

A basic principle, then, that we derive from experience is that the same set of circumstances will always be followed by the same event. But we note, also as a result of experience, that the same event is not always preceded by the same set of circumstances. I note that standing in the rain without any clothes on will always be followed by my being wet, but my being wet is certainly not always preceded by standing in the rain. I might have had a bath or bathed in the sea. Using the language of causation, the same causes will always produce the same effect, but a given effect can be the result of many different causes. As we saw in an earlier chapter, if we know that 'if p, then q' is true and we also know that q is true we can say nothing about the truth of p. So here if we know that A causes B and we know that B has happened we can say nothing about whether A has happened. My robbing a bank successfully would result in my becoming rich (at least temporarily), but from the fact that I am rich you are not entitled to deduce that I have robbed a bank. But although we are not entitled to argue from effect to cause in the same way or with the same conviction as we argue from cause to effect; although we may recognise that the same causes—if they

133

really are the same—will always be followed by the same effects, whereas the same effects may follow from many different sets of causes, nevertheless in practice we very frequently do argue from effect to cause and often with a considerable degree of conviction. We find the milk on the doorstep and argue that the milkman must have come, for after all how else could it have got there? Experts will say that a given set of fingerprints could only have been produced by one man. The business of crime detection, as readers of detective stories know very well, is mainly a matter of arguing with varying degrees of conviction from effects to causes. We know what happened. Kawps has been brutally murdered, Bogle's bicycle has been stolen. But *how* did it happen, what was the preceding chain of events?

We will never get complete certainty in inferring causes from their effects, but in practice neither can we get complete certainty in predicting effects from causes, for we can never be sure that the complete set of causes or circumstances really is exactly similar, or that some other event or cause will not intervene. This lack of certainty is clearly a matter of degree. How likely is it that the milkman setting out on his rounds really will deposit a bottle on my doorstep? When I find it there how certain can I be that it really was put there by the milkman? This very important question of probability or degree of certainty is one to which we shall return in the next chapter.

Let us now consider briefly how in practice we set about tracing the cause or causes of a given effect.

There's a rattling noise in the car—very irritating—we want to stop it. It might be one of the doors, one of the windows, the ash tray, the locker, a safety belt, or it might come from the engine. All these objects have a certain freedom of movement and one of them, or possibly more than one, is abusing it by making this awful noise. We all know what we would do. We would restrict the freedom of movement of each item in turn by holding on to it, and thus hope to eliminate possible causes. If we find that when we hold the window firmly the rattling noise still goes on, we know that at least the window cannot be entirely responsible. But if we find that the noise stops it looks as though the window is the culprit. If we could be sure that the situation, except for our holding on to the window, was exactly the same we could be certain of it. And we might be-

134

come more sure of this by repeating the experiment several times. If we find that causes p, q, r, s together produce effects a, b and that causes p, q, r, s, t together produce effects a, b, c then we can be theoretically certain that t is responsible for, is the cause of, c. We should have to say 'theoretically' because to talk about p, q, r, etc. as separate causes and to imply that we can be sure there are no others is inevitably an artificial and a theoretical thing to do.

Notice that we want to look for the factor that is always absent when the effect is absent. To look for the factor which is always present when the effect is present may lead us to true conclusions, and in practice often does. But it is theoretically unsound because it assumes that the cause must be unique, whereas in fact, as we have seen, many different causes can produce the same effect.

Suppose for example that one day I find that 'No petrol and a thunderstorm' are followed by my car not starting. The next day I find that 'A flat battery and a thunderstorm' are followed by my car not starting. The factor which is present on both occasions is a thunderstorm, but from our knowledge of cars, petrol, batteries and thunderstorms, we conclude that it would be foolish to think that the thunderstorm is the cause of my car not starting. If the causes and effects are anonymous we are much more likely to make this sort of mistake. Suppose for example that we are told that A, B are followed by p, and B, C are followed by p, we might be tempted to suppose that B, because it is common to both, is the most likely cause.

We consider now an artificial example which we make a closed system problem by assuming separate simple causes which are always followed by the same effects with nothing allowed to intervene. In spite of its artificiality this should help us to understand the mechanism of causal links.

Suppose that P, Q, R, S and x, y, z stand for simple events. We assume that a single one of the events P, Q, R, S is sufficient to cause a single one of the events x, y, z. And we assume also that the same cause will always produce the same effect, that if P causes y on one occasion it will always cause y, but that the same effect may be produced by different causes, that P and R may each separately produce y.

(Running out of petrol will *always* cause the engine of my car to stop, but it may stop also for other reasons.)

We are told that

1. P, S are followed by x, z
2. Q, R   ,,   ,,   x, y
3. P, R   ,,   ,,   y

What can we say about causal links?

Consider x first.

From 3, neither P nor R could be the cause of x, for if they were x would have followed.

In 1 therefore S must have caused x since we know that P did not. And in 2 Q must have caused x since R did not.

Therefore Q and S both cause x.

Consider y.

From 1 neither P nor S can be a cause of y. In 3 R must be a cause of y since P can't be. In 2 we know that R is a cause of y, but it is possible that Q is also; we can't be sure.

Consider z. From 2 neither Q nor R can be a cause of z, and from 3 P cannot be either.

Therefore from 1, we see that S and only S can be the cause of z.

It is important to follow this example carefully and notice the technique. If we want to trace the cause of x we direct our attention first to the situations where x is absent, and we then know that none of the factors in these situations could have caused x. (Try to find a situation where the rattling noise has *stopped*.) Situations where x is present are less informative, for any of the factors in the situation could be a cause. (Studying the situation in which the rattling noise continues is not going to help so much.)

Exercises

9.3. There is a rattling noise in my car. I have reason to be-, lieve that from only one of the two doors, one of the two, windows, the sliding roof, or the ash tray.

I fix the left window and the right door and the rattle continues.

I fix the ash tray and both windows and the rattle continues.

I fix the right door, the sliding roof and the ash tray, and the rattle stops.

What can you say about the cause of the rattle?

9.4. Lying in bed on a windy night I hear an intermittent high-pitched squeak and a regular dull thud.

I get out of bed, clasp with one hand the woogle which hangs outside my wardrobe, with the other the chumph which is loose on the top of my chest of drawers, and steady with my foot the pollux which is normally free to move round the floor on castors. The thud stops, but the squeak continues.

I keep hold of the chumph, seize with my other hand the Venetian blind, and transfer my foot to the rocking chair. The squeak stops and there is still no thud.

I now keep hold of the Venetian blind, seize the woogle once more, and take my foot off the rocking chair. The thud starts up again, but there is still no squeak.

To what conclusions should I come about the causes of the two noises?

9.5. A, B, C, D, p, q, r, stand for events. It is known that p, q, r have as their causes single events, though it is possible for p, say, to be caused by either A or B, and it is possible for C, say, to be the cause of p and q.

A, B are followed by p, q
A, C, D „ „ q, r
B, D „ „ p.

What can you say about the causes of p, q, r?

9.6. Notation and assumptions as in the previous question:

A, B, D, are followed by p, r, s
B, C, E „ „ q, r
A, D, E „ „ p, s.

What can you say about the causes of p, q, r, s?

9.7. The following is an extract from *The Adventures of Sherlock Holmes* by Sir Arthur Conan Doyle:

'I did not gain very much, however, by my inspection. Our visitor bore every mark of being an average commonplace British tradesman, obese, pompous and slow. He wore rather baggy grey shepherds' check trousers, a not overclean black frock-coat, unbuttoned in the front, and a drab waistcoat with a heavy brassy Albert chain, and a square pierced bit of metal dangling down as an ornament. A frayed top hat, and a faded brown overcoat with a wrinkled velvet collar lay upon a chair beside him. Altogether, look as I would, there was nothing remarkable about the man save his blazing red head, and the expression of extreme chagrin and discontent upon his features.

'Sherlock Holmes's quick eye took in my occupation, and he shook his head with a smile as he noticed my questioning glances. "Beyond the obvious fact that he has at some time done manual labour, that he takes snuff, that he is a Freemason, that he has been in China, and that he has done a considerable amount of writing lately, I can deduce nothing else." '

Suggest possible evidence for Sherlock Holmes's deductions. (This is not necessarily included in the description. Notice that what he is doing is to argue from the effects which he sees, to causes at which he guesses.)

9.8. Another extract from the *Adventures of Sherlock Holmes*:

' "I can see nothing," said I, handing it back to my friend.

' "On the contrary, Watson, you can see everything. You fail, however, to reason from what you see. You are too timid in drawing your inferences."

' "Then, pray, tell me what it is that you can infer from this hat."

'He picked it up, and gazed at it in the peculiar introspective fashion which was characteristic of him. "It is perhaps less suggestive than it might have been," he remarked, "and yet there are a few inferences which are very distinct, and a few others which represent at least a strong balance of probability. That the man was highly intellectual is of course obvious upon the face of it, and also that he was fairly well-to-do within the last three years, although he has now fallen upon evil days. He had foresight but has less now than formerly, pointing to a moral retrogression, which, when taken with the decline of his fortunes, seems to indicate some evil influence, probably drink, at work upon him. This may account also for the obvious fact that his wife has ceased to love him."

' "My dear Holmes!"

' "He has, however, retained some degree of self-respect," he continued, disregarding my remonstrance. "He is a man who leads a sedentary life, goes out little, is out of training entirely, is middle-aged, has grizzled hair which he has had cut within the last few days, and which he anoints with lime-cream. These are the more patent facts, which are to be deduced from his hat. Also, by the way, that it is extremely improbable that he has gas laid on in his house." '

Suggest possible reasons for Sherlock Holmes's conclusions, and consider how certain they are likely to be.

9.9. Assumptions as for *9.5.*

P, Q are followed by a, b, c
Q, R, S ,, ,, a, d
P, R ,, ,, b, c, d
a, c ,, ,, x, y
b, d ,, ,, z
a, b, d ,, ,, x, z

You have it in your power to prevent any of the events P, Q, R, S. Find the least that must be done by way of prevention to ensure that x does not happen, y does not happen, z does not happen. Justify your answers.

9.10. Sherlock Holmes speaks:

' "... I assure you that beyond obvious facts that you are a bachelor, a solicitor, a Freemason, and an asthmatic, I know nothing whatever about you."

'Familiar as I was with my friend's methods, it was not difficult for me to follow his deductions, and to observe the untidiness of attire, the sheaf of legal papers, the watch-charm, and the breathing which had prompted them. Our Client, however, stared in amazement." '
(From *The Return of Sherlock Holmes.*)

Consider how well founded Sherlock Holmes's deductions are. Can you suggest alternative explanations, or other possible causes of the effects which he sees?

CONCOMITANT CHARACTERISTICS

We referred earlier in the chapter to some cases of characteristics which are frequently found together. These are sometimes called *concomitant* characteristics. It will often be a matter of importance and interest to consider whether there is a causal link connecting these characteristics with each other or with some other factor.

(There was a very easy exercise on this in the first chapter, *1.21.*)

Suppose, for example, that someone said: 'Most jockeys are bow-legged.' If we were checking this to see whether it was true it would be reasonable to take 'most' to mean 'at least more than half', but it might not be easy to lay down a definition of what it is to be bow-legged. Let us assume, however, that this has been done and that we find that 62 per cent of the jockeys in this country are bow-legged. Before we started to search for causal links it would be sensible to discover approximately what proportion of people who were not jockeys were bow-legged. If, from a random sample, we found that the figure was about 60 per cent there would obviously be no reason to suppose that there was a causal link. But if we found that the figure was 10 per cent, that very many more jockeys than non-jockeys are bow-legged, we would certainly think that there must be a connection. And if we found that the figure was 90 per cent, that many fewer jockeys than non-jockeys are bow-legged, we would again want to find a reason.

If six times as many jockeys as non-jockeys are bow-legged we feel that it can hardly be due just to chance, that the difference is so great that it must mean something, or, to use a technical adjective, that it is *significant*. How great the difference has to be to count as significant is obviously a difficult question. Mathematicians will produce more or less precise answers as to the differences which would qualify, to use their phrase, as *statistically significant*. We do not propose, however, to go into this question here; we shall use the word 'significant' with the rather loose meaning that it ordinarily has.

When considering the extent to which characteristics are found together one is said to be examining the *correlation* between them. If it were the case that six times as many jockeys as non-jockeys were bow-legged we would say that there was a *significant correlation* between being a jockey and being bow-legged. We shall find this a useful phrase.

The figures that I have quoted above are entirely hypothetical and I do not know what the facts are. The association between being a jockey and being bow-legged is a traditional one and there is clearly no difficulty about suggesting a causal link. It is worth noticing, however, that in addition to the obvious possibility that the habitual riding of horses may be responsible for a tendency to become bow-legged, there is also the possibility that a natural bow-leggedness may help a man to ride better and therefore make it more likely that he will become a jockey.

Let us consider another example. Suppose that in a certain community there is a significantly high correlation between having gastric ulcers and being rich. What sort of causal link might there be? It is not likely that anyone would want to argue that having gastric ulcers makes one rich, but it is probably arguable that the high living which great wealth makes possible might produce gastric ulcers. It might also be argued that the way of life that leads to the accumulation of riches, a life lived at high pressure with much strain and worry, is also the way of life that is likely to lead to gastric ulcers.

The possibility that two characteristics which are found significantly often together may neither of them be due to each other, but both to a common cause, is one that is sometimes overlooked. A classic example of the possibility is to be found in the case of smoking and contracting cancer of the lung. It has been discovered that a significantly large proportion of sufferers from cancer smoke cigarettes. It looks therefore as though there is a causal link. The view that is now most generally held is that smoking is at least a contributory cause of cancer. But it has also been argued that perhaps some people have a hereditary predisposition to lung cancer and that these same people may be of the type that is more likely to smoke cigarettes. It could still be true that smoking is also itself a contributory cause.

We often in fact find that the causal link may operate in more than one direction. Suppose, for example, that it is discovered that there is a significantly high correlation between being a member of the London Stock Exchange and playing golf. It might be that some members play as a result of joining the Stock Exchange, perhaps they found that almost everyone else did and they were persuaded to join a club. Others may have become members of the Stock Exchange as a result of contacts they made playing golf. And it can probably be argued that a significantly large proportion both of members of the Stock Exchange and of golf players come from a comparatively affluent background, so that both the characteristics may in part be caused by another factor.

A great deal of investigation goes on today into the reasons for the behaviour and characteristics of various groups. Most of it comes under the description of Social Science or Sociology. Investigators in these fields are continually discovering significant correlations and attempting to explain them, that is to find out in what way, if at all, causal links operate. Obviously in doing this it is desirable that there should be a clearcut definition of the characteristics that are being considered (exactly what counts as 'bow-legged'?), and there must also be a thorough investigation into the significance of the correlation, which means, of course, that there must be a large number of examples considered. In our ordinary day-to-day living we often make generalisations from an inadequate number of examples and, by implication, attribute significantly high correlation with undefined classifications and insufficient investigation. It is important to keep a sense of proportion about this. We do not need or want to apply tests for scientific accuracy to all the casual remarks we make. It is often said for example that fat people are good-tempered, but I doubt whether this has ever been thoroughly tested. It would clearly not be an easy thing to do. It would be possible to define 'fat' in a clearcut way, but very difficult indeed to define 'good-tempered'. This would provide a very good example of the act of measurement affecting what is being measured, for it would be likely that the tests that would be necessary to discover whether people are good-tempered would themselves make their tempers less good.

For ordinary purposes we are content to leave remarks like this not very clearly defined, untested, and supported only by a limited number of personal observations. If it matters whether it is true or not, then, of course, a more careful investigation would be desirable, but it is not easy to think of any purpose for which it would be important to know whether there really is a significantly high correlation between being fat and being good-tempered.

It is perhaps also worth making again the point that sometimes when we seem to be saying that there is a significantly high correlation between two characteristics it may be to some extent a matter of definition, an analytic statement. If I say, 'Most gentlemen have good manners', it would be likely that part of my definition of being a gentleman is to have good manners—in itself a difficult characteristic to define. And it would also be likely that a purpose for which this sentence was used would be to urge people, probably the young, to behave nicely and thus to qualify as gentlemen.

9.11. For each of the following statements consider:
(a) Whether it is true.
(b) Whether it is likely to some extent to be a matter of definition, i.e. analytic.
(c) Whether the correlation can be measured (are the characteristics clearly defined?)
(d) Whether, if the correlation can be measured, it is likely to be significantly high. (If you think you *know* this, what is your evidence?)
If the answer to (d) is Yes, consider the nature of the causal link.
1. Most Spaniards are dark-eyed.
2. Most juvenile delinquents come from bad homes.
3. Most Scots are thrifty.
4. Most progressive schools are coeducational.
5. Most successful business men are methodical.
6. Most Englishmen play cricket.
7. Most British soldiers have short hair.
8. Most Conservatives in this country come from the richer half of the community.

SUMMARY
1. It is important to see what open system thinking is for: to decide upon the worthwhile ends and how to achieve them.
2. For this purpose we want to understand how the world works; how events are causally connected.
3. When we want to know how things work we ask *why* or *how*. The answer to 'why' questions can either be in terms of purpose (a final cause), or in terms of preceding events (an efficient or a mechanical cause). This distinction may be difficult to uphold on a close analysis.
4. The causal link is something that in general we take for granted as a result of our experience. If we want to discover whether it exists in particular cases we must be aware of the facts (which again are derived from experience), that the same set of causes will always produce the same effects, but the same effects may be the results of many different sets of causes.
5. This means that in theory one can argue with certainty from

causes to effects (what will follow from certain events), but not from effects to causes (what preceded or was responsible for certain events).

6. But in practice, in an open system, causes are seldom (or never), precisely the same, and a great deal of argument takes place with varying degrees of certainty both from causes to effects and also from effects to causes.

7. Characteristics which are frequently found together are sometimes called *concomitant*. It may be a matter of importance to discover whether their association is sufficiently frequent for there to be a *significant correlation*, and if so to find the nature of the causal link, if any.

Chapter 10

Probability, Prediction and Control

In the first chapter when we were considering Mrs Jones's problem of when to go shopping we talked about her balancing the probabilities and desirabilities. A word that we frequently use, and which has appeared very often in this book is 'likely'; it is more or less a synonym for 'probable'. We wonder how 'likely' it is that something will happen; we talk about one event being 'more likely' than another. We all know, at least roughly, what we use these words to mean, but it will be worth while now to give the whole idea of Probability a rather closer scrutiny.

MATHEMATICAL DEFINITION OF 'PROBABILITY'

We start with a very simple example to illustrate the mathematical definition of 'probability'. I toss a coin. It would be agreed that if it is a normal coin tossed under normal conditions it would be equally likely to come down heads or tails. For the moment we propose to take the idea of 'equal likelihood' for granted, though we shall be looking at it more closely later. The probability of its coming down heads is said to be 1/2, or the chances of its coming down heads are said to be even. If we throw a die with six faces numbered 1 to 6 in conditions where all the faces are equally likely to come uppermost we would say that the probability of throwing any one of the numbers is 1/6, or that the chances of throwing any one of the numbers are 5 to 1 against. Obviously, according to this definition, if there are 100 equally likely events the probability of any one of them occurring is 1/100 and the chances against it are 99 to 1.

A complicated and interesting mathematical theory of probability has been erected on this basically simple assumption of the probability of equally likely events. The complexity of it derives usually from the problem of the number of different ways in which things can happen, the number of possibilities for example when a die is thrown several times or when several dice are thrown.

Let us consider a few simple examples. Suppose that I toss a coin twice and want to know what the probability is that it will come down heads at least once. The possibilities for the two throws are as follows (using H and T to denote Heads and Tails respectively):

$$H, T; H, H; T, T; T, H$$

These four possibilities are equally likely; in three of them H comes at least once. Therefore the probability of the coin coming down heads at least once is 3/4, or the chances are 3 to 1 in favour.

If the coin we tossed was heads on both sides we would say that the probability of its coming down heads was 2/2 or 1. This is another way of saying that it is a certainty, or that it must necessarily happen. But we can obviously only say this if such possibilities as its balancing on its edge or disappearing in a hole in the ground are not to be allowed to count.

On the assumption therefore that the events we are considering are of a kind such that they must either happen or not happen, that no other possibility is allowed, we can deduce that if the probability of something happening is, say, 1/6, the probability of its *not* happening is 5/6 (1–1/6). As we have just seen, if something is certain or necessary its probability is 1, and on our assumptions it is certain that (or necessary that) the event either will or will not happen.

In the example about the coin, therefore, from the fact that the probability of its coming down heads at least once in two throws is 3/4 we can deduce that the probability of its not coming down heads at least once, in other words of its coming down tails both times, is 1/4. This conclusion could also have been arrived at more simply by seeing that the combination T, T is one of the four possibilities.

If a die is thrown twice it is easy to see the number of different possibilities. One for the first throw can be followed by any of the six numbers for the second throw, similarly 2 can be followed by any of the six numbers and so on. Altogether therefore there are 6×6 or 36 different possibilities. (If a die were thrown three times the number of possibilities would be 6×6×6.) The probability therefore of throwing two sixes on consecutive throws is 1/36. And the probability of throwing, say, first a 2 and then a 5 would also be 1/36. It is worth noticing, however, that if two dice are thrown simultaneously although the probability of throwing two sixes would still be 1/36 the probability of throwing a 2 and a 5 would be 1/18, for this combination can be obtained in two ways, either by one die being 2 and the other 5 or vice versa.

From what has been said it is clear that if there are two independent events of which we know the probabilities, the probability of them *both* happening will be obtained by multiplying the probabilities together. If we throw a die and toss a coin the probability of the die showing a 3 is 1/6, and of the coin showing tails is 1/2; the probability of the die showing 3 *and* the coin showing tails is therefore 1/12. (It would be easy to check this by writing down all the possibilities.)

When there are two events which cannot both happen, for example the same die on a given throw showing 2 and showing 4, the probability of *either* one *or* the other happening will clearly be obtained by adding the probabilities together. (In this case 1/6 +1/6=1/3). It is not so easy, however, to see the probability of *either* one event *or* the other happening when they can happen together. Suppose in the example above we want to find the probability of *either* the die showing 3 *or* the coin showing tails. It would seem natural to add the probabilities (1/6+1/2=2/3), but this would involve a double reckoning, counting twice the occasion when they both occur. We should therefore subtract the probability of their both occurring and we get as our answer: 1/6+1/2−1/12=7/12 (The reader may like to convince himself of this by writing down all the 12 possibilities for a die and a coin and and seeing that in 7 of them *either* the die shows 3 *or* the coin shows tails or both.)

It is important to realise that the idea of probability which we are here talking about is one that is defined with mathematical precision in a closed system. It depends on the assumption—necessarily a closed system one—of equally likely events. It must not be confused, as it often is, with our expectations, though the theory will often tell us a great deal that is useful about what it is reasonable to expect. If in throwing a die we found that it showed 5 on ten consecutive occasions, it might be thought that it surely couldn't happen next time, that because it had happened ten times running the probability must be less for the next throw. In fact, of course, if the events are equally likely the probability is exactly the same, 1/6, and what has happened before is irrelevant. The probability is exactly the same because that is the definition of probability. As an alternative it might not unreasonably be supposed, not that the probability of a 5 is *less* than 1/6, but that it is *more*. The fact that 5 has turned up ten times running might lead us to suspect that the die is loaded, that there is some trick, that the events in fact are not equally likely.

We do not propose to go further into the mathematical theory of probability, though it has been important to give the reader some idea of what it is about. Below are some simple exercises on the points we have discussed. In order to pursue the matter further it would be necessary to know more about how to calculate the number of ways in which events can happen, for example the number of different ways in which three cards can be selected from a pack of 52. This is dealt with in mathematical textbooks under the heading of Permutations and Combinations.

Exercises

10.1. I toss a coin and throw a die. Find the probability of: (i) 4 and heads; (ii) a number greater than 4 and heads; (iii) an odd number and tails; (iv) either 5 or tails or both.

10.2. Two dice are thrown one after the other. What is the probability of the first showing a 2 and the second a 3? If they were thrown together what would be the probability of their showing a 2 and a 3?

10.3. A coin is tossed four times. What is the probability of its showing heads: (i) once only; (ii) at least twice; (iii) four times?

10.4. Two dice are thrown together. What is the probability of their showing either a 4 or a 5 or both?

10.5. Two dice are thrown together. What is the probability of the total of the two faces being: (i) exactly 8; (ii) 8 or more?

10.6. A bag contains 10 marbles which are all of the same size, weight and texture. One of them is white, 3 are red and 6 are black. There are 13 cards numbered 1 to 13, face downwards on the table.

With one hand I draw a marble from the bag, and with the other I turn up a card.

What is the probability of:

(i) a red marble and a six

(ii) a black marble and a three

(iii) neither a black marble nor a two

(iv) neither a white marble nor an even number

(v) either a white marble or a four or both

(vi) either a red marble or a seven but not both?

10.7. I toss a coin and throw two dice. What is the probability of:

(i) a double six and heads

(ii) a double six or heads or both

(iii) a double six or heads but not both

(iv) a three and a five and tails

(v) at least one of: a three, a five, tails?

10.8. (i) How many people must be collected together for it to be certain that at least two of them have their birthdays on the same day?

(ii) How many times must you throw two dice to be certain of getting a double six?

(iii) How many dice must you throw to be certain that at least two of them will show the same?

(iv) How many people must be collected together for it to be certain that at least two of them are the same age?

(v) Ten pairs of shoes in a cupboard. How many shoes must you take out to be certain of getting at least one pair?

10.9. There are four pink cards numbered 1 to 4, and three blue cards numbered 1 to 3. If you draw one of each what is the probability of the total being: (i) greater than 5; (ii) exactly 5?

(iii) If the number of pink cards is still four how many blue cards (numbered consecutively, starting at 1) must there be for it to be more likely than not that the total of two cards, one of each colour, shall be 5 or more?

EQUALLY LIKELY

We will now examine more closely the phrase 'equally likely'. If

149

we were asked what we meant by saying that a coin when tossed was equally likely to show heads or tails we might answer by producing a synonymous phrase ('just as probable'), or, more convincingly, we might give either the reason why we say it or the test of its truth. The reason why we say it, is that when we examine the coin we can see nothing about it that will tend to make heads come uppermost rather than tails or vice versa; there is no factor to weight our prediction one way or the other. And therefore we think that if it were tossed a very large number of times it would show heads and tails equally often or very nearly so. This is the test that 'equally likely' is true and in part an explanation of its meaning.

Mathematicians who are dealing with probability theory would define 'equally likely' in rather more formal terms by saying that the greater the number of times an unbiased coin was tossed the more nearly would the proportion of heads tend to be equal to the proportion of tails. We usually find when we toss a coin several times that heads and tails appear about equally often (I have just tossed a penny 100 times: 56 heads, 44 tails). If they do not we may have doubts as to whether the coin was really unbiased, whether the two were equally likely. But there are many pitfalls and difficulties about this. Suppose, for example, that a coin is being tossed an indefinitely large number of times, that is for ever and ever. The mathematicians would tell us that at some stages in the proceedings, even if the coin is unbiased, there will be runs of, say, 30 consecutive heads. If we happen to come in at the beginning of one of these and find the coin showing heads 30 times running we might need some convincing about the lack of bias. There is an inevitable circularity about our definitions and terms here. We say that an unbiased coin is likely in the long run to come down heads and tails approximately equally often. If an experiment seems to show this not to be true are we to say that the coin could not after all have been unbiased, that the events were not equally likely or that the run was not long enough? There is no simple answer to these questions. In fact there is some rather deep water here in which it will be wise not to get too far immersed. It will be sufficient for our present purposes if we make the following points.

1. The test for equal likelihood of events is whether they happen equally often in the long run. This test can never be completed. No run can be long enough in theory, though most people would be

prepared to accept the evidence provided by, say, tossing a coin 100 times as sufficient to make them feel fairly sure.

2. But it is clearly a difficult matter to decide by just how much heads must exceed tails or vice versa for us to feel that it cannot be due to chance. Most people would probably feel that 56 heads and 44 tails could perfectly well be due to chance, but would feel exceedingly doubtful as to whether 90 heads and 10 tails could be. The mathematicians will have an answer. They will be prepared to tell us how great the deviation from equality will have to be to count as significant. They tell us in fact how surprised it is reasonable to be. But it is important to realise that there is no question of their being able to tell us that because the odds against 100 consecutive heads are astronomically high (or the probability very low) therefore it cannot happen.

In fact, as the reader will be able to deduce from previous examples, the probability is 1 in 2^{100}. This is obviously very small.[1] But it is exactly the same as the probability of heads and tails occurring in just the order in which they did occur when I tossed a penny recently and got 56 heads and 44 tails. You might toss a coin continuously for many millions of years before getting a precise repetition of that sequence. The odds against it were astronomically high. But it happened. (This is not to say, of course, that 56 heads and 44 tails are 'as likely' as 100 heads. Very many different sequences will produce 56 heads, but only one out of the 2^{100} sequences will produce 100 heads.)

3. We are sometimes told that things happen according to the 'Laws of Chance'. These 'laws' are simply the principles of the mathematical theory of probability. They may be very useful in telling us what to expect and how surprised to be if it doesn't happen. They may enable us to make predictions with great confidence, almost with certainty. But, as we have already seen, in the world of contingent events we can never be quite certain.

4. We have already noted the inevitable circularity of the definition of 'equally likely'. It is important to note too that events to which the phrase can be applied are few and limited. When we toss coins, throw dice, play cards, roulette or other games of chance we can often reasonably talk about events being equally likely. But these

[1] 1 in 1267650600228229401496703205376.

on the whole are rare and artificial events and are frequently arranged merely to demonstrate the idea of 'equally likely' and the theory that is based on it.

Since the theory of probability depends on the assumption of equally likely events and since these events are in practice infrequent it is obvious that the applications of the theory are inevitably limited.

LIMITATIONS OF MATHEMATICAL THEORY OF PROBABILITY

When we say that the odds are 5 to 1 against an unbiased die showing 3 when thrown, this is a matter of definition. Nothing is being said about anybody's expectation, and we cannot be proved wrong by what happens when the die is thrown. If someone else says they are 6 to 1 he is wrong; he just cannot know or understand how mathematical odds are defined.

But supposing I say that I reckon the odds are 5 to 1 against its raining here this afternoon. In this case I am clearly saying something about my expectations; I feel reasonably confident that it will not rain. If it does rain, my prediction is incorrect. I was, in a sense, wrong to feel confident. Was I wrong also in saying that the odds were 5 to 1 against? It is hard to see how one can maintain that there is an answer to this unless one also maintains that there is an answer to the question as to what the odds really were, as there certainly was with the die. But is there any sense in which with the weather one can talk about a specific number of equally likely events? Is there any way in which one can make a large number of experiments with all the relevant conditions the same in order to test for equal likelihood? To ask these questions is surely to see how impossible it is to do these things and how absurd therefore to suppose that there is some definite answer as to what the odds really are.

What one can do, of course, is to study the weather, to learn about meteorological chains of cause and effect, to investigate what happened under similar conditions in the past. And the more closely one studies these things the more frequently should one be able to make a confident and correct prediction as to whether it will rain in the afternoon. It will often be interesting to make an estimate of the strength of our expectations by attaching a numerical value to them and perhaps by making a bet about it, but it does not seem sensible to talk about what the odds really are except in those cases, based on equally likely events, to which the mathematical theory of probability can properly be applied.

This is, however, a thing that we frequently do, especially when something very unexpected and unusual happens. Suppose, for example, that two cars on little-used roads (average one car an hour) approach a crossroads at right-angles to each other; the brakes of both cars fail and they collide. It might then be said that it is estimated that the odds against such a happening were millions to one. We could certainly say that each driver might reasonably feel surprised; it was a very unlikely event. But is there any sense in which a figure of what the 'odds really were' against it could have any sort of precise meaning? Given that on an average one car per hour uses each road we could start working out the probability of a car passing a particular point in a period of 5 seconds. But this would assume that all periods of 5 seconds are equally likely, whereas in fact many of the cars that use the roads do so at regular times—Mr Pringle for example going to and returning from his office. And what about the odds against the brakes failing? Shall we try to find out on how many cars per day, or per hour the brakes fail? But can we assume that they are equally likely to fail on the new Rolls Royce and on the 15-year-old, badly neglected, cheap and out-of-date model? The more closely we look at the matter the more absurd it is seen to be to start wondering just what the odds are against such an event.

But one can, of course, perfectly reasonably talk about one's expectation and of how likely one thinks it is that the event will happen. My expectation of meeting another car at the crossroads will depend on whether I happen to know that Pringle usually passes this way about now; and my expectation about the brakes failing will depend on whether I've had the car serviced recently. And, of course, if I do predict to myself that my brakes might fail and that Pringle might be passing I will take particularly good care to see that these events do not result in a crash. It is also worth noticing that my expectation, whether I am thinking about it at all, and if so how likely I judge these things to be, will depend to some extent on my temperament and on my other preoccupations at that moment.

CERTAIN AND PROBABLE

We take a look now at the words 'certain' and 'probable' and the other words that are derived from them.

'Certain' is used in two rather different ways. We may say 'I am certain', or we may say 'It is certain'. When we say 'I am certain' there is no doubt about what we mean. We are talking about our state of mind; we all know what it is like to feel sure, and there is no particular problem or difficulty about it. We may be referring to events in the past, in the present or in the future. It is obvious, however, that to feel certain about something is no guarantee that it is so. Some people will express themselves as certain much more frequently and on much slighter evidence than others, but most of us have probably had the experience of saying that we are sure and then being proved wrong.

When we say 'It is certain', we seem to be saying something different and more authoritative. We might use the phrase about something that follows necessarily; for example I might say 'It is certain that if two sides of a triangle are equal, then the angles opposite those sides are equal.' In such a case what is being said is clearly different. I am not saying anything about my state of mind or anybody else's; I am talking about necessity or logical certainty in a closed system.

The phrase, however, is frequently used also about contingent events in an open system. Suppose I say 'It is certain that it's raining outside'. In this case I would have to admit if pressed that I am only saying that *I* am certain, perhaps completely certain, and that anybody else who looked out of the window would be too. We say '*It* is certain' rather than '*I* am certain', to emphasise that it's not merely a matter of our personal opinion, that a great many other people are certain too—or would be if confronted by the same evidence. But it does not seem to be sensible to think of the certainty as being *in* the events in the same sort of way as the logical necessity is *in* the proposition about the triangle. In the latter case the necessity is there because we put it there in a way in which we cannot put certainty into events.

It is interesting that although we can say either 'I am certain' or 'It is certain', we can only say 'It is probable'. There is no use of 'probable' that corresponds to 'I am certain'. Our language is constructed in such a way that if we talk about probability at all we have almost got to imply that it is somehow *in* the events. Opinions differ as to whether it is right or sensible to think about it in this way, and this is a problem which, like many others, we can only deal with superficially here. My own opinion is that if we examine closely what we mean when we say 'probably' we will almost always find that what we are really talking about, or all that we are entitled to talk about, is our expectations. If I say that Australia will probably win the Test Match I am saying that my judgment is that they will win, perhaps that I am fairly sure they will win. I may also be implying that on the evidence available many other people are likely to have formed (which means to say that *I think* they have formed) the same judgment. Events will show whether we are right or wrong. It does not seem to me sensible to talk about probability being in the events except in the clearly defined mathematical sense of probability that we have already considered. I suggest that it will help us to think more clearly if we see that 'It is probable' or 'probably' can generally be replaced by 'It is my opinon' or 'I and many others are fairly sure.'

One of the reasons for this misleading habit of language may well be the convention, until recently fairly strictly observed, that one should not use the first person singular much in print. We therefore write 'It is probable' rather than 'I think'. This may sometimes have the effect of making pronouncements appear more authoritative than mere personal expressions of opinion. On the other hand if we make the pronouncements without either 'I think' or 'probably' or their equivalents they may appear more dogmatic and conclusive than we intend. 'Probably' is therefore very often a qualification to show that the writer does not state this as a matter of fact, that he is not quite sure about it. I am well aware that anyone who cared to count would find that 'probably' and 'it is likely' occur very often in this book.

Exercise 10.10

Consider whether it is possible to express the meanings of the following sentences without using the word 'probable' or its derivatives or synonyms. If so, rewrite them.

1. You'll probably find the cigarette box empty.
2. The probability of your throwing a double six is exactly 1/36.

3. The right policy at this juncture depends on a delicate balance of probabilities.

4. Smith is far more likely to win than Jones.

5. You're much more likely to throw a three and a four than you are to throw a double four.

6. 'The odds are probably still slightly in favour of Britain having a Labour Government in six weeks' time.' (*Economist*, 5 September 1964)

Prediction

To talk about how probable or likely things are is to indicate the degree of confidence with which we can make predictions. And one of the main reasons for understanding the world is to enable us to make correct predictions about what is going to happen next.

It is worth noticing again that as a result of dealing with the strict mathematical sense of probability and investigating the number of equally likely events in certain situations we may get much useful assistance about how confidently to predict certain happenings or how surprised to be if certain things do or do not happen. We would hardly need a study of probability theory to tell us to be very surprised indeed if, when playing bridge, we pick up a hand of thirteen spades. But when we know the contents of our own hand and our partner's it may be useful to have some idea about how likely various distributions of the remaining cards are between our two opponents. (For example if they have five hearts between them in what proportion of the possible distributions will the player on my left have all of them?) Quite often what might appear to common sense to be an amazing coincidence will be seen on examination to have quite a high probability (using the word now in its technical sense). If asked, for example, the least number of people that would have to be in a room together to make it more likely than not that two of them have their birthday on the same day, most people without experience of this type of question guess wildly wrong. (The answer is in fact 23—smaller than common sense would be likely to suppose. The mathematics is rather complicated. Anyone who feels sceptical about it might find it interesting to make the experiment of asking the next 23 people he meets the dates of their birthdays.)

The predictions that we make will be partly about inanimate objects (details about the next eclipse of the sun, for example) and partly about the behaviour of animals and human beings. An exceedingly important point about predicting what people will do is that the predictions may affect their behaviour, may make a difference in fact to what is being predicted. The classic example of a prediction making an event more likely is a city editor foretelling that the price of a certain share on the Stock Exchange will go up. If he is believed speculators will rush to buy in the hope of selling later at a profit, and the increased demand will send the price up. If, however, it is predicted that John Smith will be killed in an air accident next Tuesday he may cancel any arrangements he may have made to fly on that day. (On the other hand if he is the sort of person who doesn't believe in predictions like that and wants to demonstrate the fact, he may go out of his way to make arrangements for an air trip.) At the moment of writing there is some controversy as to whether Public Opinion Polls affect what they predict. People (or a sample of them) are asked what they are going to do (for example, how they are going to vote in the next election); they are then told what they are going to do by the publication of the result of the poll. Will this make it more or less likely that they will collectively behave as the poll predicts or will it make no difference?

Exercise 10.11

Consider whether the following predictions are likely to make a difference to what is predicted:

1. 'It is expected that waistlines will be three inches lower this year.' (A ladies' fashion magazine)
2. 'You'll drink yourself into the grave.' (Wife to husband)
3. 'Traffic to the West out of London next Friday evening is expected to reach record proportions.' (A daily newspaper)
4. 'It is expected that prices of Government securities will rise quite sharply next week.' (A daily newspaper)
5. 'It is expected that the price of petrol will go up next week.' (A daily newspaper)
6. 'You'll probably find this next question rather too difficult for you.' (Schoolmaster to his form)
7. 'It is expected that all tickets [for the cup tie] will be sold by noon tomorrow.' (A daily newspaper)

CONTROL

We want to understand and predict in order to be able to plan and to control our environment, to achieve our objectives as efficiently as possible. We want to know what is likely to happen if we take this course of action because we want to bring about X and to prevent Y. All our practical problems are concerned with causes and effects, probabilities, desirabilities. We have to decide what we want to achieve for others and for ourselves and how to do so.

The variety of problems that there are to be solved is almost endless, and to attempt any sort of detailed analysis is beyond the scope of this book.

Some general remarks, however, may be useful.

1. Individually and collectively men have first to decide what they want. Quite a large proportion of the resources of a modern nation is devoted to persuading people by advertising to want certain things, and this persuasion is clearly to a considerable extent successful. The technique is to predict the high degree of satisfaction that the customer will enjoy. The intelligent and critical citizen will examine these predictions very carefully. Will the effects really be as predicted, and if so will they be as enjoyable as predicted? Could not these effects be achieved more economically in some other way? Is there a sufficient, sensible balancing of wider long-term desirable ends against the narrow short-term advantages on which the advertiser is usually mainly concentrating?

2. The most difficult and also the most important problems are concerned with the way people behave. To ask whether the so-called nuclear deterrent will deter, is to make an enquiry about how certain people will react in a hypothetical situation. Solutions of economic problems involve mainly a consideration of what people—employers, employees, bankers, industrialists, trade union officials—will do if taxes are raised or lowered, prices go up or down, incentives are offered, rewards are increased, and so on. Ideally we want to be able to predict how people will in fact behave and to devise methods to make it more likely that their actions will be to the advantage of the community (assuming for the moment that we are more or less agreed about the answer to the question as to what *is* to the advantage of the community). These things are exceedingly difficult. It is probably the case today that a greater proportion of the community than ever before is engaged in the task of dis-

covering why people behave as they do, predicting how they will behave and devising methods for moulding or even controlling their behaviour. These people will be doctors, sociologists, economists, politicians, advertisers and others. The greater their experience and the clearer their thinking the more likely they are to get the answers right. But it is obvious that what they are doing has its dangers as well as its potential advantages.

3. One of the most effective aids to the solution of problems is to keep on asking ourselves what we are trying to do, what it's for, what is the object of the exercise. In considering rival methods of achieving this object it is clearly desirable to set out the advantages and disadvantages of each, not forgetting to include the possible long-term effects and any personal factors that may be relevant.

4. An important benefit that should result from a training in clear thinking is the ability to detect flaws in suggested solutions to problems, and in arguments generally. These flaws may take a variety of forms: a misleading use of words, a matter of taste or judgment masquerading as a matter of fact, a mistake in logical structure, an unreasonable prediction, or an erroneous assumption about the nature of a causal link. And this list, of course, does not claim to be exhaustive.

SUMMARY

1. We know roughly what we mean by 'certain', 'probable', 'likely', but it is desirable to examine the ideas rather more closely.

2. The mathematical theory of probability is based on the assumption of equally likely events. The probability of an event is the ratio of the number of ways in which it can happen to the total number of relevant equally likely events. (Twelve marbles in a bag: 3 white, 4 black, 5 yellow. The probability of a marble drawn out being yellow is 5/12.) The mathematics required to discover in how many different ways things can happen may be complicated.

3. When we examine the idea of 'equally likely' we see that we cannot in practice verify it. We have to say that things will happen equally often in the long run, and no run can ever be long enough. In a sense, therefore, it is bound to be a theoretical, closed system idea.

4. Nevertheless the results of the calculations involved in the mathematical theory of probability may be very useful as a practical guide

to what to expect; and to give us some indication as to how surprised we should be if various things do or do not happen. But we must remember that they cannot give us information that is certain. To talk about 'what the odds really are' when we are dealing with contingent events can be misleading.

5. It is suggested that when we talk about events being certain or probable we are really only entitled to talk about our states of mind, our expectations. And these, of course, depend on the evidence and our assessment of it. Except in the strictly defined mathematical sense, with the assumptions which that entails, we should not think of probability being 'in the events'.

6. Our expectations obviously determine the nature and the confidence of our predictions. We note that predictions may often make a difference to what is predicted.

7. We want to understand and predict in order to be able to tackle the various practical problems that arise. A detailed analysis of these is beyond the scope of this book. Some general remarks are made.

Miscellaneous Exercises

M.1. In reply to the suggestion that magistrates who tried motoring offences should themselves all be experienced motorists someone said: 'You might just as well say that magistrates who try cases of theft should themselves all be experienced burglars.'
Do you agree that one 'might just as well say'? Discuss.

M.2. Comment on the way in which the words in italics are used in the following passages:
1. '*Jests* that give pain are no *jests*.' (Cervantes)
2. 'We may all be able to read now, but to read rubbish is only another kind of *illiteracy*.' (R. Duncan: *Spectator*)
3. 'Must the Turtle die? Indiscriminate slaughter may wipe out a *noble* creature that, emerging before the dinosaur, has roamed the seas for 200 million years.' (*The Sunday Times*)

M.3. Consider whether in the following extract what can only be a matter of opinion is being claimed as a matter of fact:
'I ask the House to believe me that never at any time in my dealings with the trade unions... have I ever shown provocation or arrogance (Ministerial cheers). Never shall I do so.' (*The Times*, Parliamentary Report)

M.4. 'Every time road casualties increase we are told that there were more cars on the road, which is like saying, "No wonder hooliganism increases. There are more hooligans about." ' (Beachcomber: *Daily Express.*)
Is it 'like saying'? Discuss.

M.5. Comment on the following:
'There *is* no brain drain. There *are* a number of scientists who

are taking what appear to them better jobs in places that happen not to be in the United Kingdom.' (Henry Fairlie: *Spectator*)

M.6. 'It is safer to be a driver than a pedestrian in New York. Pedestrians account for 68 per cent of traffic deaths so far this year.' (*Daily Express*)
Do you think the second sentence justifies the first?

M.7. Discuss the logic of the following:
   'I was very conscious that the task I had set myself would not be short or easy, but it's a long lane that has no turning and I would therefore devote myself to the job unflinchingly until it was completed. Nor was I prepared, remembering that the best is the enemy of the good, to lower my sights in any way. Having put my hand to the plough I was not going to be persuaded by fatuous clichés such as "In for a penny, in for a pound", into looking back.
   'My friend Jorkins was anxious that I should not overwork: as he wisely remarked "A stitch in time saves nine." But I pointed out to him that what was sauce for the goose was sauce for the gander, that if Jones could do it then I could keep up with him. I find that Jorkins, though he means well and is helpful in many ways, tends to concentrate so much on the general picture that he can't appreciate the importance of the detail; in fact he can't see the wood for the trees.'

M.8. Comment on the following:
   '. . . Surely if our cars are good we shall be able to sell as many abroad as we can make and if they are not good we should not be making them at all.' (Letter to *The Times*)

M.9. Analyse the nature of the claim made in the following extract:
   'We haven't yet learned how to succeed in retailing without really trying. But we have clearly learned certain ways to success, and the one formula that never fails is to advertise the right goods—at the right time—in the right newspaper.' (Head of a New York department store, quoted in *Daily Express*)

M.10. '—— affirmed . . . that "the general shape of our law is good and the tasks for reform are limited". The contrary is the truth: the general shape of our law is bad and the tasks for reform are immense.' (*The Sunday Times*, leading article on Law Reform)

Do you think that 'contrary' is being used in its correct logical sense? Explain and justify your answer.

M.11. Discuss the logic of the following extract from a political speech:

'—— is reported as saying that he wanted to carry out his plan as a military operation ... the demand for a military operation is the theme song of the dictator from time immemorial. The characteristic of military operations is the disregard of human happiness and rights ... The appearance of efficiency which ruthlessness requires is a pure illusion. It is freedom and democracy which are efficient, in spite of appearances to the contrary.' (Mr Quintin Hogg as reported in *The Times*.)

M.12. Comment on the argument implied in the following letter. Do you think it is reasonable?

'Sir, The Prison Commission is advertising for prison officers at the princely starting pay of £11 18*s*. per week. This is about the sum it costs to keep either a man or woman in prison, and about £3 less than it costs to keep a person in a Detention Centre or Borstal. What's wrong with our sense of values?' (Letter to *The Observer*)

M.13. 'The air I breathe is the condition of my life, not its cause.' (Coleridge)
Explain clearly the implied distinction.

M.14. Explain, analyse and discuss the argument implied in the following letter to *The Times*)

'Sir, In your leading article today you describe as "drastic" the limitation of car production as a solution to the overcrowding of our roads. You also say it is "thoroughly undesirable" and wrong.

'However, on page eight of the same issue, the limitation of baby production as a solution in the fight against overpopulation is reported as having "hope of greater success".

'This I feel, Sir, is a sad comment on our present-day sense of values.'

163

M.15. ' "Jones reads Karl Marx; Communists read Karl Marx; therefore Jones is a Communist" is as false as saying "Groucho Marx eats
fish; cats eat fish; therefore Groucho Marx is a cat".' (Katherine
Whitehorn: *The Observer*)
Do you agree that it is 'as false'?: (a) considered as a formal argument in a closed system; (b) considered as a piece of reasoning in an
open system, in which other, unstated, premisses may be used?

M.16. Consider the following argument:
'You are always complaining of melancholy, and I conclude from
those complaints that you are fond of it. No man talks of that which
he is desirous to conceal, and every man desires to conceal that of
which he is ashamed.' (Dr Johnson in a letter to Boswell)

M.17. An author complains:
'Consider a copy of my book being sold in a bookshop. The
transaction takes only a few minutes. Yet the profit which the book-
seller makes on the sale is larger than the amount which comes to
me in royalties. If you think of the years of hard work that went
into that book the distribution of the proceeds is obviously grossly
inequitable.'
Do you think his complaint is justified? Discuss.

M.18. 'Mr ——'s suggestion, in his letter on 4 September, if a lorry
is found to be in a dangerous condition the head of the owning firm
should be liable to a term of imprisonment appears to be a good one.
It is obviously wrong that the driver should be held wholly responsible if he has reported the danger.
'Does it not, however, follow logically from this that if a place
on a trunk road has, by repeated accidents, shown itself to be
dangerous the Minister of Transport should be equally liable to a
term of imprisonment.'
Do you agree that it follows logically? Discuss.

M.19. 'The real issue was a simple one: how many immigrants—
black, brown, white or yellow—can we, in these islands, provide
with jobs, rooms or houses, transport, places in schools for their
children and hospital beds? Obviously there's a practical answer.

164

It can't be as high as a million or as low as none. Somewhere between the two lies an answer.' (Elspeth Huxley, *Punch*)
Does it seem to you to be reasonable to say that somewhere between the two *lies an answer*? Discuss.

M.20. The following is an extract from a letter to *The Times* from an Oxford don:

'I may add that we are also blamed for taking too much of the intellectual cream of the country. [The first thing for which they were blamed was the 'enrolment of athletes and aristocrats without an idea in their fat heads'.] If we gave equal weight to these contradictory complaints we should stand, like Buridan's Ass, immovable between two bundles of hay.'

Do these two complaints seem to you to be contradictory? Is the metaphor of Buridan's Ass an apt one?

M.21. In August 1964 there was considerable correspondence in *The Times* about the Electricity Board's proposal to erect pylons in an area of West Sussex that was considered particularly beautiful.

Below are extracts from some of the letters:

1. 'This piece of countryside is, for intrinsic quality and its location in desperately overcrowded south-east England, one of the most precious we have. World famous, it does not belong to Sussex alone. To let this be destroyed for the sake of £15m. ... seems hardly credible. Comparing the figure with what is spent on projects like Blue Streak or the Concord aeroplane, it is clear that estimates of national priorities need revision.'

2. 'This wanton damage to landscape by the proposed erection of these monstrous giants makes absurdity of the years of patient endeavour by landowners, county and district authorities, parish councils and a host of voluntary organisations to protect from eyesore some of the finest scenery left in Britain today.'

3. 'The Ministry's inspector ... was quite powerless to pronounce on the much larger question at issue—namely, whether the rape of the Downs was necessary at all ...'

4. ' "I wish that pylons were not necessary and that we could put

the lines underground. Unfortunately that is impossible", Sir Christopher Hinton, Chairman of Central Electricity Board, as reported in your issue of August 21.

'Impossible? In an age that spends millions on space research and contemplates the probability of putting men on the moon!'

5. 'The telegraph poles that once ran down our roads used to give me immense pleasure (dare I say aesthetic pleasure?) as do still many of man's defacements of the earth's natural surface: the fresh-ploughed fields, the farmsteads, the steeples, the viaducts, even the chalk-pits. The telegraph poles have vanished, almost. Will our children one day regret the passing of the pylons?'

6. 'I wonder if any of your correspondents who write so passionately about pylons have ever really looked at them. Sitting at lunch on a Welsh mountain today, my son and I saw them as a graceful addition to the landscape . . .

'I love the South Downs as much as any of your correspondents can do . . . But I should think it blind, not to say selfish, to suggest that the pylons on them have even begun to spoil their beauty, any more than agriculture has. . . .

'How some of your correspondents would have loathed Edward I for erecting his monstrous castles round Snowdonia! How ugly they would have found the first windmills! . . .'

7. 'If one was to engage in a certain amount of research I am sure we would find the evidence . . . of the seventeenth and eighteenth centuries campaigning against the building of those monstrosities, the windmill, which mar the Sussex landscape.

'And I am more than sure that the John Betjemans of the twenty-first and twenty-second centuries will still be campaigning for the preservation of the pylons which carried that ancient form of power to the homes of their forebears.'

8. 'Mr —— [the writer of letter No. 6] misses the essential difference between windmills or castles and electricity transmission lines. The former have through their materials and functions a close relationship with their setting and increase the sense of locality. The latter have no such relationship with their setting and represent an extension of mechanised industry into the countryside and detract from the sense of locality.'

9. 'One of your correspondents [letter No. 7] . . . brings my name into a letter likening pylons to windmills.

'May I point out the falsity of his analogy? Windmills would never be put underground. Windmills never marched in straight lines from a central generating station. Windmills were hand made and not all of a pattern and some were probably more worth preserving than others.

'It is sentimental to glorify pylons. We all really know why pylons are to be allowed to industrialise and change the character of downs and modest agricultural landscape far more effectively than ever will our new and well-landscaped motorways. The reason is money. Since we live at a time when money is regarded as more important than aesthetics we must expect the electricity undertakings to continue to ruin country districts with overhead wires and cables.'

10. '. . . It came as a shock to learn that some crass bureaucrat has approved plans to wreck forever this precious heritage—one of the few remaining features of England that has no equal, anywhere in the world.'

11. 'It seems odd to me that we hold up our hands in horror at the sight of pylons on the march and at the same time view the new Forth Bridge with wide-eyed admiration.'

(a) 1 and 4 both make the point that considering the sums of money we seem to be prepared to spend on other projects it ought to be possible to put the lines underground. Which letter seems to you to make the more convincing comparison? Give reasons.

(b) How effective do you think 8 is as an answer to the last paragraph of 6?

(c) What exactly is the point that is being made by 7? Do you think that the second paragraph of 9 successfully disposes of it?

(d) Analyse what is meant and what is involved by saying that 'we live at a time when money is regarded as more important than aesthetics.' (Letter No. 9.) Give reasons for agreeing or disagreeing.

(e) Discuss the emotive use of words or phrases in these letters.

(f) Many of these letters explicitly describe the attitude of the writer. Do there seem to you to be any words or phrases by which an attitude or a matter of personal taste is represented as being something else—for example a matter of fact or a matter of generally agreed opinion?

(g) On which side of the argument does it seem to you that greater passion is displayed? Discuss why this should be so.

(h) With which side do you find yourself in greater agreement? Why?

M.22. Analyse the following:
'Extremism in the defence of liberty is no vice ... moderation in the pursuit of justice is no virtue.' (Senator Goldwater.)
Do you agree?

M.23. Five people A, B, C, D, E are related to each other. Four of them make statements as follows:
1. B is my father's brother.   3. C is my son-in-law's brother.
2. E is my mother-in-law.   4. A is my brother's wife.

Each person who is mentioned is one of the five (e.g. when some-one says 'B is my father's brother' you can be sure that 'my father' as well as 'my father's brother' is one of A, B, C, D, E).
Find out who made each of the four statements and exactly how the five people are related.

M.24. A, B, C, D, E, F, G are arranged in a certain order (no ties) as the result of a competition. Statements are made as follows:
1. E was 2nd or 3rd.   5. B was not first.
2. C was not 4 places higher   6. D was not 3 places lower
than E.   than E.
3. A was lower than B.   7. A was not 6 places higher
4. B was not 2 places lower   than F.
than G.
Only two of these statements are true. Which? Find the order.

M.25. Seven nurses A, B, C, D, E, F, G have a day off every week, no two of them on the same day.
You are told that A's day off is the day af   C's; that D's day off is three days after the day before E's; that B's day off is three days before G's; that F's day off is half way between B's and C's and is on a Thursday.
Which day does each nurse have off?

M.26. Work schedules and personalities in the Utopia Factory are strange and complicated.

In order to avoid friction and advance production certain rules are drawn up for the five employees, Alf, Bert, Charlie, Duggie and Ernie.

These rules are as follows:

1. If Alf is present Bert must be absent unless Ernie is absent, in which case Bert must be present and Charlie must be absent.
2. Alf and Charlie may not be present together or absent together.
3. If Ernie is present Duggie must be absent.
4. If Bert is absent Ernie must be present unless Charlie is present, in which case Ernie must be absent and Duggie must be present.

In a certain five-day week it was observed that the combination of those present was different every day; it was also observed that Alf and Ernie were present the same number of times as each other but less often than anyone else.

Who were present on the different days of the week?

M.27. There has been a fever of excitement at the Utopia Factory about the forthcoming election.

The Managing Director goes round in person to ask how they're all going to vote. They answer and then go on to say one or two other things.

Every statement made by the Liberals is true.

Every statement made by the Communists is false.

The Socialists make statements which are alternately true and false, starting with a true statement.

The Conservatives make statements which are alternately false and true, starting with a false statement.

Their names are Alf, Bert, Charlie, Duggie, Ernie, Fred, George, and their jobs, not necessarily respectively, are Door-Knob-Polisher, Sweeper-Upper, Door-Opener, Door-Shutter, Worker, Welfare Officer, Bottle-Washer.

They make statements as follows:

ALF. 1. I shall not vote Communist or Socialist.

2. None of us belong to the same party as Bert.

BERT. 1. I shall not vote Conservative.

2. George is a Liberal.

CHARLIE. 1. I shall vote Communist.

    2. Duggie belongs to the same party as the Bottle-Washer.

    3. The Welfare Officer is not a Communist.

DUGGIE. 1. I shall vote Liberal.

    2. Bert is a Conservative.

ERNIE. 1. I shall vote Conservative.

    2. George's party is different from the Door-Opener's.

    3. Alf is the Door-Knob Polisher.

FRED. 1. I shall not vote Socialist.

    2. The Sweeper-Upper is a Conservative.

    3. Alf and the Worker belong to different parties.

GEORGE. 1. I shall vote Socialist.

    2. Duggie is a Communist.

Find their jobs and their political parties.

M.28. In the days when there were only five employees in the Utopia Factory their names were Alf, Bert, Charlie, Duggie and Ernie, and their jobs were—not necessarily respectively—Door-Keeper, Door-Knob-Polisher, Bottle-Washer, Welfare Officer and Worker.

The question arose as to whether, and if so what, they should be paid. It was clearly very difficult to arrange things in such a way that merit should be appropriately rewarded, but eventually, after much thought, I, as Managing Director, put up the following notice:

PAY

1. Alf is to get more than Duggie.

2. Ernie is to get 12 per cent more than the Bottle-Washer will when he receives the 10 per cent rise that he will be getting next month.

3. The Door-Knob-Polisher is to get 30 per cent more than he used to.

4. Charlie is to get 12*s.* less than 20 per cent more than the Welfare Officer.

5. No one is to get less than £10 or more than £30 per week.

6. The Door-Keeper is to get 5 per cent more than he would if he got 10 per cent less than Bert.

7. Everyone heretofore, now and hereinafter, has received, does receive and will receive, an exact number of shillings per week.

170

What are the various jobs of my employees and what weekly wage is each of them to get?

M.29. Alf, Bert, Charlie, Duggie, Ernie, Fred and George, have been smitten with a mysterious disease. They have all been admitted to the sumptuously appointed sick bay, and have been given the private rooms numbered 98–104, which are consecutively situated round the central circular hall.

Those of them whose temperatures are under 99° never tell the truth unless they are wearing pink pyjamas, in which case they make statements which are alternately true and false.

Those of them whose temperatures are over 102° have seen the light (red) and always tell the truth.

Those of them whose temperatures are between 99° and 102° inclusive make statements which are alternately true and false.

Two of them are wearing pink pyjamas, and the colours of the pyjamas of the other five are flame, blue, green, yellow and aquamarine.

(Anyone who is known to make statements which are alternately true and false may start in the statements below with one which is either.) They make statements as follows:

ALF. 1. Fred's pyjamas are aquamarine.
    2. Charlie's room number is 2 greater than his temperature.
    3. Duggie's room number is over 100.
BERT. 1. Alf's room number differs by 3 from Fred's temperature.
    2. Duggie's temperature is 100°.
    3. George's temperature is 98°.
CHARLIE. 1. Fred's temperature is 98°.
    2. Ernie's room number is even.
    3. Fred is wearing blue pyjamas.
    4. I am not wearing yellow pyjamas.
DUGGIE. 1. Alf's pyjamas are green.
    2. My temperature is greater than my room number.
    3. Alf's temperature is one less than his room number.
    4. My pyjamas are flame.
ERNIE. 1. My pyjamas are pink.
    2. My temperature is under 99°.
    3. Bert's temperature is 2° higher than Fred's.

171

FRED. 1. My temperature is not 101°.

2. Duggie's room number is a prime.

3. Charlie's temperature is over 102°.

4. Bert's and Ernie's rooms are next door to each other.

GEORGE. 1. My pyjamas are not pink.

2. Charlie's temperature is 97°.

3. Charlie's temperature is over 102°.

4. The number of Fred's room is 2 greater than the number of Bert's.

Find for each of them his room number, the colour of his pyjamas, and as nearly as possible, his temperature.

Acknowledgements

We are grateful to the following for permission to reproduce copyright material:

The British Iron and Steel Federation (advertisement); the *Daily Express* for the article 'Free to Spend' from the issue dated 7 September 1964; the *Daily Telegraph* for an extract from an article by Peter Simple from the issue dated 11 February 1964; the Trustees of the Estate of Sir Arthur Conan Doyle and John Murray (Publishers) Ltd. for extracts from *The Adventures of Sherlock Holmes* by Sir Arthur Conan Doyle; *The Times* for extracts from issues dated 4 and 6 December 1963.